THE JOHN HARVARD LIBRARY

The John Harvard Library, founded in 1959, publishes essential American writings, including novels, poetry, memoirs, criticism, and works of social and political history, representing all periods, from the beginning of settlement in America to the twenty-first century. The purpose of The John Harvard Library is to make these works available to scholars and general readers in affordable, authoritative editions.

JOHN
HARVARD
LIBRARY

THOMAS PAINE

COMMON SENSE

INTRODUCTION BY ALAN TAYLOR

JOHN
HARVARD
LIBRARY

THE BELKNAP PRESS OF HARVARD UNIVERSITY PRESS

Cambridge, Massachusetts, and London, England   2010

Library of Congress Cataloging-in-Publication Data

Paine, Thomas, 1737–1809.
Common sense / Thomas Paine ; introduction by Alan Taylor.
p. cm. — (The John Harvard Library)
Includes bibliographical references.
ISBN 978-0-674-05116-4 (pbk.)
1. United States—Politics and government—1775–1783.
2. Political science—United States—History—18th century.
3. Monarchy.   I. Title.
E211.P1455 2010
973.3—dc22   2010017364

Contents

Introduction

ALTHOUGH WAR BETWEEN British troops and American Patriots began in April 1775, the Continental Congress dared not declare independence for fear of the divisions among the colonists. A strong American minority opposed any military resistance to British rule. These Loyalists had a healthy respect for the British military prowess, a deep appreciation of the commercial benefits of the empire, and a dread that a revolution would dissolve law and order. They detected impending anarchy in the Patriot mobs that used violence to intimidate the Loyalists. In addition, the Patriots were divided into moderate and radical camps. Like the Loyalists, the moderate Patriots dreaded the British military might, valued the stability and prosperity that the empire had so long provided, and feared mob violence. Unlike the Loyalists, however, the moderate Patriots hoped to tame the popular fervor by leading it. While willing to resist the British forces, the moderates still hoped for a reconciliation with British rule. If Parliament would withdraw its troops and cancel its colonial taxes, the moderates were ready to restore their royal governors and once again submit to British regulation of their foreign trade. But radical Patriots sought a dramatic break with Britain by declaring independence and by adopting a republic that would dispense with a king and an aristocracy.

Americans had long believed that the British mixed constitution of king, lords, and commons provided the most stable and freest government possible for human beings. Colonists found confirmation in the military success and commercial prosperity of the British Empire, which had triumphed over the French and the Spanish in the Seven Years' War of the late 1750s and early 1760s. Beginning in 1764, Parliament sought to pay for the expanded military by imposing new taxes on the colonies without seeking approval from their elected assemblies. By resisting the new taxes, the colonists sought to preserve their privileged place within a prospering empire. Only when war erupted in 1775 did some Patriots begin privately to consider independence, and most Americans still dreaded any public discussion of separation from Britain. On December 6, 1775, the delegates of the Continental Congress renewed their allegiance to the king, limiting their opposition to abuses by Parliament. Thomas Paine later noted that the colonists' "attachment to Britain was obstinate, and it was at that time a kind of treason to speak against it . . . and their single object was reconciliation."[1]

In late 1775 in Philadelphia, prominent radicals sought a writer who could swing public support in their favor. Led by Dr. Benjamin Rush of Philadelphia, they recruited Paine, an immigrant who had arrived the year before from England. Hard-drinking, self-educated, and restlessly ambitious, Paine had accomplished little in the previous thirty-seven years of his checkered life. Born in the English country town of Thetford in Norfolk County in 1737, Paine was the son of a Quaker corset-maker. Young Paine learned and followed that same low-paying artisanal trade, interrupted by a brief wartime stint as a privateer. Seeking better pay and higher status, in 1762 he secured an appointment as an excise tax collector. Disappointed in the income, he turned to writing and published his first pamphlet, *The Case of the Officers of Excise*, in 1772 in London, but his plea for higher salaries failed to move Parliament. Worse still, in 1774 the government dismissed Paine for neglecting his duties. That year his marriage to Elizabeth Ollive, a shopkeeper's daughter, also crumbled. Separating, they sold their paltry household possessions at auction to pay their debts. At rock bottom personally, Paine emigrated to the American colonies in desperate search for a new start. Frustrated by his experiences with the class hierarchy of Britain, Paine longed to find a land that would favor ingenuity rather than the privileges of birth.

In November 1774, he arrived in Philadelphia, the leading seaport in British America even though its population barely topped 30,000. This commercial city thrived by exporting the wheat and flour produced by the hinterland farms. Instead of titled aristocrats, the city's elite consisted of merchants, lawyers, and land speculators. Although he was impressed by the prosperity, Paine found the colonies in an uproar over the "Coercive Acts" imposed by Parliament to compel obedience to its taxes and to its troops. Alienated from Britain by his own experiences, Paine quickly threw in with the Patriot resistance. Thanks to a letter of introductions from Benjamin Franklin, another former tradesman, Paine became the executive editor of the *Pennsylvania Magazine* in January 1775. By embracing the Patriot cause, Paine more than doubled the magazine's subscriptions during the spring and summer.

His forceful writing won the admiration of Dr. Rush, who encouraged Paine to publish a pamphlet against reconciling with British rule. But Rush also urged Paine to write indirectly, avoiding two words "by every means as necessary to his own safety and that of the public—*independence* and *republicanism*." Of course, Rush underestimated the headstrong Paine's political zeal and eagerness for confrontation. An Englishman with a record of failure would try to persuade Americans to gamble their lives and properties on independence and republicanism.[2]

In early December, Paine completed his manuscript and submitted it to his friends Rush, David Rittenhouse, and Benjamin Franklin, who all approved. On January 10, 1776, in Philadelphia, Paine published *Common Sense*, which became the most powerful and pivotal pamphlet in American history. A Scottish-born printer, Robert Bell, published the first one thousand copies. Although the edition sold out within two weeks, Paine felt cheated in the proceeds, so he turned to another Philadelphia firm, that of William and Thomas Bradford, who produced another six thousand copies. Paine then dedicated his profits to buying mittens for the Patriot soldiers, but those profits largely vanished, because the colonies lacked a copyright law, and almost every Patriot press in the colonies quickly reprinted *Common Sense*. Paine later estimated that American presses sold at least 150,000 copies, a phenomenal total for a public of only three million people, a fifth of them illiterate slaves. Many more colonists read long excerpts from *Common Sense* in their local newspapers, and the illiterate heard it read aloud in taverns and streets. Except for the Bible, no written work had ever been so widely read and discussed in America. Initially, *Common Sense* appeared anonymously, but by March many Americans knew that Thomas Paine was the author.

In *Common Sense*, a writer found his moment to change the world. Unlike previous political pamphleteers who wrote in a learned and legalistic style, Paine directly addressed common voters with limited education. Thomas Jefferson marveled, "No writer has exceeded Paine in ease and familiarity of style, in perspicuity of expression, happiness of elucidation, and in simple and unassuming language."[3] Seeking a broad audience, Paine wrote in clear, direct, and concise terms, and he employed vivid but common metaphors and analogies. Paine later explained, "As it is my design to make those that can scarcely read understand, I shall therefore avoid every literary ornament and put it in language as plain as the alphabet."[4] Rather than dwell on the words of arcane political philosophers, Paine quoted only from the Bible—the primary text known and revered by his intended readers. For Paine, style was also substance, for he sought to recruit and to constitute a new readership: a broad and engaged public for a republican revolution. Appealing to readers of common learning and sense, Paine insisted that they should no longer defer to guidance by their supposed betters: "Notwithstanding the mystery with which the science of government has been enveloped, for the purpose of enslaving, plundering and imposing upon mankind, it is of all things the least mysterious and the most easy to be understood."[5] Aptly titled, *Common Sense* sought to speak both to and for the common people of America and the world.

Common Sense pushed for immediate American independence, a union of the thirteen resisting states, and republican governments for the states in that union. All three concepts represented a dramatic break with past experience and received wisdom. No colonies in the Americas had yet broken free from their mother empire; the British American colonies had a track record of bickering and prejudices that augured poorly for a union; and almost all past republics had been small, contentious, and short-lived. Conventional thinking insisted that American colonies needed a European protector in a dangerous world, that any union of the thirteen colonies would quickly collapse into a civil war, and that a republic would dissolve into a violent anarchy without a king and an aristocracy to check and balance the volatility of the common people. In a stroke of daring genius,

Paine argued that the Americans could triumph by *combining* the three gambles: independence, union, and republic. Seeking one alone would certainly fail, but the *combination* would prove irresistible. If none of his particular ideas were original, the package was.

Above all, Paine sought to create a republic. He later explained that independence would have been hollow if the American "government had been formed on the *corrupt models of the old world.* It was the opportunity of *beginning the world anew* . . . of bringing forward a *new system* of government in which the rights of *all* men should be preserved that gave *value* to independence." An avid student of natural science, Paine insisted that common people could and should remake their governments to escape from exploitation by the wealthy and wellborn.[6]

To vindicate a republic, Paine needed to destroy the American reverence for the mixed constitution and for the reigning king, George III. Blaming Parliament for the taxes, the Patriots had long looked to the monarch as a potential ally, for he represented the revered union of the empire. To free Americans from that tradition, Paine denounced king and aristocrats as vicious frauds who duped and exploited working people. By dispensing with such parasites, common folk could, at last, live free and prosper. Paine declared, "all men being originally equals, no one by birth could have a right to set up his own family in perpetual preference to all others." He concluded, "of more worth is one honest man to society, and in the sight of God, than all the crowned ruffians that ever lived." And George III was "the Royal Brute" responsible for killing Americans and "with their blood on his soul." By discrediting the sovereign king, Paine made independence thinkable—as he relocated sovereignty from a royal family to the collective people of a republic. Parliament receded in importance as the king became the great villain in a republican crusade for an independent union.[7]

Paine also had to shatter the American respect for the power of the British Army and the Royal Navy, and he needed to bolster the shaky confidence of Americans in their own military abilities. In early 1776, Loyalists and moderate Patriots feared that prolonged fighting would destroy scores of towns and thousands of lives in a futile struggle against an irresistible empire. Countering those doubts, Paine insisted that, if united, the Americans could not lose a war for independence and a republic. Blessed by a righteous cause, they would fight with a virtuous resolve that would overwhelm the corrupt mercenaries of a royal tyrant. "'Tis not in numbers but in unity that our great strength lies, yet our present numbers are sufficient to repel the force of all the world," Paine declared.[8]

Finally, Paine cast the American struggle in utopian and universal terms. By winning republican self-government, the Patriots could achieve an ideal society of perpetual peace, soaring prosperity, and an egalitarian distribution of property and of political rights. America offered the world's last, best hope for liberty and equality:

> Every spot of the world is overrun with oppression. Freedom hath been hunted round the globe. Asia and Africa have long expelled her. Europe regards her like a stranger, and England hath given her warning to depart. O! Receive the fugitive, and prepare in time an asylum for mankind.

By proving that a republic could thrive, Americans would inspire common people throughout the world to free themselves from their kings and aristocrats. He concluded, "The cause of America is in a great measure the cause of all mankind . . . The birth-day of a new world is at hand."[9]

Today Americans take this soaring rhetoric for granted, but it was new and radical for colonists who had long felt self-conscious about their parochial and provincial status. Paine relocated them from the colonial margins of a sophisticated empire to the center of a new and coming world of utopian potential. He invested their cause with the global and millennial meaning essential to motivate the immense sacrifices needed to win a revolutionary war against a mighty empire. Far less could be expected of people engaged in a pedestrian drive to remain within the empire but without taxation by Parliament. "The sun never shined on a cause of greater worth," Paine concluded.[10]

Common Sense outraged and alarmed Loyalists. Traveling through Virginia, Nicholas Cresswell wrote in his diary: "A pamphlet called 'Commonsense' makes a great noise. One of the vilest things that ever was published to the world. Full of false representations, lies, calumny and treason whose principles are to subvert all Kingly Governments and erect an Independent Republic."[11] Troubled by the pamphlet's popularity, Loyalists hastily responded with their own pamphlets, principally *Plain Truth* by James Chalmers of Maryland, who defended the mixed constitution as "the pride and envy of mankind."[12]

Common Sense's emotional tone and popular appeal also alarmed some moderate Patriots. Elias Boudinot of New Jersey denounced Paine as a "Crack Brain Zealot for Democracy." Gouverneur Morris of New York disliked Paine as "a mere adventurer . . . without fortune, without family or connexions, ignorant even of grammar." Elitists worried that Paine would whip up a popular fervor for revolution that would undermine the traditional authority of men with prestigious family connections. Wealthy gentlemen like Boudinot and Morris led Congress and its Continental Army, but the revolution also relied on thousands of common men as rank-and-file soldiers, junior officers, state legislators, and local committeemen. That reliance troubled the gentry, who worried that the common people might demand sweeping changes in the distribution of property and power.[13]

But Paine enabled many Americans to overcome their fears of revolution and independence. In vivid and forceful prose, Paine gave focus to previously inchoate longings for conviction. After reading the pamphlet, Joseph Hawley, a Patriot leader, aptly remarked, "Every sentiment has sunk into my well-prepared heart." In Connecticut, a Patriot marveled to Paine, "You have declared the sentiments of millions . . . We were blind, but on reading these enlightening words the scales have fallen from our eyes." The Patriot general Charles Lee wrote to his superior, General Washington, "Have you seen the pamphlet *Common Sense?* I never saw such a masterly irresistible performance."[14]

Timing favored *Common Sense,* for the British outraged many moderates by escalating the war, burning Falmouth in Maine and Norfolk in Virginia. With hopes for reconciliation fading, George Washington predicted that "a few more of such flaming arguments as were exhibited at Falmouth and Norfolk, added to the sound doctrine and unanswerable reasoning contained in the pamphlet *Common Sense,*" would soon induce Congress to choose independence. In the America of early 1776, Paine found the ideal conjunction of place and time and audience for his radical ideas and polemical abilities.[15]

By the spring of 1776, Patriots noted a decisive swing in public opinion. Although about a fifth of the people remained Loyalists committed to the union of the empire, a clear majority expected Congress to declare independence. In early June, Richard Henry Lee of Virginia introduced a resolution in favor of independence and union. To draft a declaration, Congress chose a committee which included Benjamin Franklin of Pennsylvania, John Adams of Massachusetts, and Thomas Jefferson of Virginia. The most gifted writer of the three, Jefferson produced the fundamental draft which owed much to *Common Sense,* particularly the focus on human equality and on damning the king to justify independence. The declaration ignited mobs who systematically destroyed symbols of monarchy, tearing down and burning the royal arms posted on public buildings and tavern signs.

Patriots wrecked New York City's great equestrian statue of George III and melted its parts to make bullets to shoot at the British troops.

But winning independence proved far trickier than destroying royal symbols. In July 1776, Paine joined General Washington's army as the aide first to General Daniel Roberdeau and later to General Nathanael Greene. Routed by the British, the Patriot army retreated in disarray across New Jersey to Pennsylvania in late 1776. While Loyalists exulted, many Patriots despaired. To bolster their morale, Paine wrote the first of his *American Crisis* essays in December:

> These are the times that try men's souls: The summer soldier and the sunshine patriot will, in this crisis, shrink from the service of his country; but he that stands it now, deserves the love and thanks of man and woman. Tyranny, like hell, is not easily conquered; yet we have this consolation with us, that the harder the conflict, the more glorious the triumph.[16]

Once again, Paine donated his royalties to the military cause of revolution. Paine's words helped Washington to rally enough volunteers to mount a desperate Christmas Night counterattack which captured Trenton, New Jersey, routing the garrison of British-employed Hessian mercenaries. Between 1777 and 1783, Paine would issue twelve sequels to the *American Crisis* to rally public support for the war effort.

Meanwhile, on the home front, the Patriots struggled to craft constitutions for their thirteen states and for a unifying confederation of those states. That constitutional process reignited tension between the moderate and the radical Patriots, who fought over the proper form of a republic. Paine and other radicals sought simple state constitutions, easily understood and worked by common people directly to express their desires. They preferred a unicameral legislature, annual elections, term limits for legislators, low or no property requirements to vote or to hold office, and no governor to check the legislature. While Paine served in the Continental Army, his political allies drafted and secured just such a democratic constitution for Pennsylvania, which he vigorously defended in published essays.

The moderate Patriots preferred complex state constitutions that restrained the democratic potential of common voters. While conceding the need for a popular role in elections, the moderates distrusted common people as easily misled by selfish demagogues. By conducting a tyranny of the majority, such demagogues would (the moderates predicted) prey upon the property of the wealthy minority. To hem in democracy and demagogues, the moderates wanted to require substantial property to vote and to hold office. They also sought to check and balance a popular assembly with an elitist state senate and a powerful governor. Although a radical for independence, John Adams was a moderate in his constitutional views. In 1776, he derided Paine's plan of government, presented in *Common Sense,* as "so democratical without any restraint or even an attempt at any equilibrium or counterpoise, that it must produce confusion and every evil work." Ultimately, the moderates prevailed in Pennsylvania, remaking the state constitution in 1790 to provide for a governor and a bicameral legislature.[17]

Meanwhile, in 1783 the British made peace and recognized the United States of America as a sovereign nation. But the new nation suffered from the weak confederation government established in 1781. Although most radicals favored a decentralized confederation where most political power remained with the states, Paine promoted a new federal constitution with a stronger national government, which became fruition in 1788.

A year before, Paine had embarked for Britain to seek investors to build his innovative design for a wrought-iron bridge. Like other eighteenth-century radicals, Paine combined an interest in politics, science, and technology. By discovering the principles of order in nature, these men hoped to craft new machines and new constitutions: both meant to improve the conditions of common people by rescuing them from the related burdens of poverty, ignorance, and tradition. A devout believer in progress, Paine insisted that the world stood on the brink of a new age of greater prosperity, equality, liberty, and knowledge.

Unable to find investors for his bridge, Paine instead became embroiled in another republican revolution, which erupted in France in 1789. Embracing that cause, Paine published in 1791–1792 the two-volume *Rights of Man*, which again ridiculed the monarchy and aristocracy of the British Constitution. Promoting a republican meritocracy for Britain, he concluded, "It is an age of revolutions, in which every thing may be looked for."[18] Once again, Paine caused a sensation, selling thousands of copies and inspiring a widespread reform movement led by merchants, shopkeepers, and artisans. To suppress that movement, the British government banned *Rights of Man* and indicted Paine for sedition.

Fleeing to France, Paine won election to the National Convention and joined the vote to abolish the French monarchy. But in this revolution, he favored the relatively moderate Girondin faction, which opposed the execution of the king and the queen. During the summer of 1793, the Girondins lost power to the more radical Jacobins, who arrested and executed thousands of their rivals and foes. In December 1793, the Jacobins arrested Paine and cast him into Luxembourg Prison. After narrowly dodging execution, Paine won his release in November 1794.

He remained in France for another seven years, which he dedicated to an ambitious program of controversial publications. In 1794–1795, he published, in two installments, *The Age of Reason*, which he had begun while in prison. Championing the rationality of science, this new work denounced organized religion and biblical miracles

as frauds perpetuated by priests and aristocrats to dupe and to ex-
ploit the common people. Rejecting all church creeds, Paine declared,
"I believe in one God, and no more . . . I believe in the equality of
man; and I believe that religious duties consist of doing justice, loving
mercy, and endeavouring to make our fellow-creatures happy."[19] His
anti-biblical stance broke with his reverential use of the scriptures to
support his argument in *Common Sense* nearly twenty years before.
He followed up, in 1795, with *Agrarian Justice,* which urged a redistribution of wealth by taxes to fund a welfare state that could educate
the poor and support the elderly. And in 1795 and 1796, he sent to
America for publication two blistering open letters to the American
president, George Washington, the champion of the Federalist party.
Paine blasted his former friend as a treacherous hypocrite who had
failed to push for Paine's immediate release from prison in France.

In 1801, Paine's political friend Thomas Jefferson won election to
the American presidency; a year later Paine returned to America to
a mixed reception. Jefferson and his fellow Republicans initially wel-
comed Paine and celebrated his role in the revolution. But Paine had
made many new enemies, particularly among the Federalist party,
with his attacks on organized Christianity and the beloved Washington. One Federalist newspaper called him a "lying, drunken, bru-
tal infidel," and another denounced "the loathsome Thomas Paine,
a drunken atheist."[20] Feisty as ever, Paine poked back by publishing
essays to mock Federalists and to ridicule scriptural religion. Those
publications embarrassed mainstream Republicans, including Jefferson, who increasingly kept their distance. Drinking more heavily,
Paine bitterly complained that Americans were ingrates who had for-
gotten his immense services to their independence and freedom.

Consigned to obscurity and poverty, he died on June 8, 1809, in
New York City. Only six mourners attended his funeral. Ten years
later, William Cobbett, an English radical, crossed the Atlantic to un-

earth Paine's corpse and to take it to England for reburial beneath a new monument. But Cobbett died without building the memorial, and Paine's bones became lost, apparently forever.

Even Paine's greatest critics could not deny his enormous influence on an age of transatlantic revolutions. The most trenchant critic was John Adams, who claimed that Paine had stolen too much credit for promoting American independence. On the one hand, Adams dismissed *Common Sense* as "a poor, ignorant, Malicious, short-sighted Crapulous Mass," and on the other, he insisted that Paine had lifted his best ideas from Adams's speeches in Congress. But even in his contempt, Adams had to concede the power of Paine's influence, writing in 1805,

> I know not whether any man in the world has had more influence on its inhabitants or affairs for the last thirty years than Tom Paine. There can be no severer satyr on the age. For such a mongrel between pigs and puppy, begotten by a wild boar on a bitch wolf, never before in any age of the world was suffered by the poltroonery of mankind to run through such a career of mischief. Call it then the Age of Paine.

Adams raged that Paine had aroused a common public in America, Britain, and France to reject the traditional expertise of learned men.[21]

Throughout his life Paine struggled to help the poor and the middling folk to escape exploitation by aristocrats and kings. In 1806, he explained, "My motive and object in all my political works, beginning with *Common Sense* . . . have been to rescue man from tyranny and false systems and false principles of government, and enable him to be free."[22] Privileged by law and government, aristocrats and bishops were titled parasites who preyed on the enterprise of common people through taxes, tithes, and rents. Paine favored the classical liberalism of John Locke and Adam Smith, who had a greater confidence in the market than in the aristocratic government of their century. Eighteenth-century liberals hoped that a truly free market would favor the abilities and industry of common people, creating a more equal and just society of small-scale producers: farmers, shopkeepers, and tradesmen. If broadly distributed among most families, private property could empower common people to defend their rights against entrenched elitists. A classic liberal, Paine imagined society as fundamentally a free market "composed of distinct, unconnected individuals, following various trades, employments and pursuits; continually meeting, crossing, uniting, opposing and separating from each other, as accident, interest, and circumstances shall direct."[23] But he ultimately believed that a free commerce between small producers would provide a common bond "of mutual and reciprocal interest."[24]

A man of his time, Paine never anticipated our modern economy where men of fabulous wealth now seek freedom from government regulation so that their multinational corporations can dominate global flows of capital and may set the terms of labor. Today most people cannot enter the market as independent, small-scale producers, as Paine envisioned in his ideal society. Unable to own their own farm or shop, most people must instead labor as employees for capitalist firms or government bureaucracies.

The past two centuries of social and economic change have obscured the nature of Paine's radicalism. Latter-day conservatives, including Glen Beck, Sarah Palin, and Ronald Reagan, selectively quote Paine as the champion of minimal government, low taxes, entrepreneurial enterprise, and laissez-faire economics. They delight in repeating Paine's insistence that "society in every state is a blessing, but government even in its best state, is but a necessary evil."[25] But they do not mention that Paine also denounced military establishments and Christian fundamentalism, or that he ultimately championed a redistribution of wealth by a welfare state that would equalize inheritance and would fund public education and old-age pensions. Flexible in his strategies, Paine remained true to his fundamental goal of seeking greater freedom through greater equality for all. In the past century, competing ideologues have divided Paine's message, offering people either freedom or equality rather than both.

Notes

1. Philip Foner, ed., *The Complete Writings of Thomas Paine* (New York: Citadel Press, 1945), 1:143–144.

2. Benjamin Rush to James Cheetham, June 17, 1809, quoted in John Keane, *Tom Paine: A Political Life* (Boston: Little Brown, 1995), 104.

3. Thomas Jefferson quoted in Keane, *Tom Paine*, 114.

4. Paine quoted in Eric Foner, *Tom Paine and Revolutionary America* (New York: Oxford University Press, 1976), 83.

5. Ibid., 85n22.

6. P. Foner, *Complete Writings*, 2:957.

7. Ibid., 1:13–16, 29.

8. Ibid., 1:31.

9. Ibid., 1:3, 30–31, 45.

10. Ibid., 1:17.

11. Nicholas Cresswell, *The Journal of Nicholas Cresswell, 1774–1777*, 2nd. ed. (New York: Dial Press, 1924), 136.

12. James Chalmers quoted in Keane, *Tom Paine*, 125.

13. Elias Boudinot quoted in Larry Gerlach, *Prologue to Independence: New Jersey in the Coming of the Revolution* (New Brunswick, N.J.: Rutgers University Press, 1976), 485; Gouverneur Morris quoted in P. Foner, *Complete Writings*, 1:xviii.

14. Joseph Hawley quoted in E. Foner, *Tom Paine*, 86; *Connecticut Gazette*, March 22, 1776, quoted in Winthrop D. Jordan, "Familial Politics: Thomas Paine and the Killing of the King, 1776," *Journal of American History* 60 (1973): 29; Charles Lee to George Washington, Jan. 24, 1776, quoted in Keane, *Tom Paine*, 111.

15. George Washington quoted in E. Foner, *Tom Paine*, 86.

16. P. Foner, *Complete Writings*, 1:50.

17. John Adams quoted in Keane, *Tom Paine*, 126.

18. P. Foner, *Complete Writings*, 1:344.

19. Ibid., 2:1434–1438.

20. Boston's *Mercury and New-England Palladium* and Philadelphia's *Port Folio*, quoted in Harvey J. Kaye, *Thomas Paine and the Promise of America* (New York: Hill and Wang, 2005), 91.

21. Lyman H. Butterfield, ed., *Diary and Autobiography of John Adams* (Cambridge, Mass.: Harvard University Press, 1961), 3:333; Lester J. Cappon, ed., *The Adams-Jefferson Letters* (Chapel Hill: University of North Carolina Press, 1959), 542; John Adams to Benjamin Waterhouse, Oct. 29, 1805, quoted in Adrienne Koch and William Peden, eds., *The Selected Writings of John and John Quincy Adams* (New York: Alfred A. Knopf, 1946), 148.

22. P. Foner, *Complete Writings*, 2:1480.

23. Paine quoted in Isaac Kramnick, *Republicanism and Bourgeois Radicalism: Political Ideology in Late Eighteenth-Century England and America* (Ithaca, N.Y.: Cornell University Press, 1990), 154.

24. Paine quoted in E. Foner, *Tom Paine*, 93.

25. Paine, *Common Sense*, in P. Foner, *Complete Writings*, 1:4–5.

Note on the Text

IT WAS AT THE STRONG urging of his friend Dr. Rush that
Paine, acting through a go-between, engaged the Philadelphia
bookseller and printer Robert Bell to publish *Common Sense*. A letter
of agreement specified the printing of one thousand copies and equal
division of any profits between the anonymous author and Bell. Paine
had always intended his share of the profits to be used for the pur-
chasing of mittens for the Patriot forces fighting in Quebec. Published
on January 10, 1776, *Common Sense* proved an immediate success. Bell
was already planning to reprint the pamphlet when the relationship
between author and publisher soured. Paine was furious to learn the
first printing had produced no profits. Believing he had been cheated,
he quickly entered into a new agreement with the rival Philadelphia
firm of William and Thomas Bradford to produce an enlarged edition. An acrimonious quarrel ensued in the pages of the *Pennsylvania
Evening Post*. Paine strengthened his work and increased its appeal by

adding new material (Appendix and "Address to the Quakers") to the Bradford edition. To expedite publication, William and Thomas Bradford contracted two printers, the shop of Benjamin Towne, publisher of the *Pennsylvania Evening Post,* and the newer shop of Melchior Styner and Charles Cist. Bell, meanwhile, proceeded with his own second edition. The expanded Bradford edition appeared on February 14, 1776. The publication history of *Common Sense* becomes more complex at this point, because Paine forfeited copyright and allowed other publishers to reprint the work free of charge. By Paine's own calculations, 120,000 copies had been sold in the first three months of its publication, and one contemporary biographer places the number as high as 500,000 copies at the end of the first year. Collation reveals that the Benjamin Towne printing of the expanded Bradford edition is more accurate than the Styner and Cist. The John Harvard Library edition follows the text of the Towne printing. A detailed account of the publication of *Common Sense* can be found in Richard Gimbel's *Thomas Paine: A Bibliographical Check List of* COMMON SENSE *with an Account of Its Publication* (New Haven, Conn.: Yale University Press, 1956).

Chronology of Thomas Paine's Life

29 January 1737   Born Thomas Pain in Thetford, England, the son of Joseph Pain and Frances Cocke.

1750   After seven years at the Thetford Grammar School, Paine begins an apprenticeship with his father as a corset-maker.

1757   Serves for seven months on the privateer *King of Prussia* during the Seven Years' War against France.

1757–1758   Works as a journeyman corset-maker in Dover and visits London to attend popular lectures on Newtonian science.

1759   Moves to Sandwich to open his own corset shop and to wed Mary Lambert, a domestic servant.

1760   Mary Lambert Paine dies in childbirth.

1762   Paine appointed excise tax collector in Lincolnshire.

1765   Dismissed from the excise service for filing a false report; resumes his trade as a corset-maker in London, where he also sporadically teaches school.

1768   Restored to the excise service and assigned to Lewes, on the Channel Coast.

1771   Marries Elizabeth Ollive, the daughter of a Lewes shop-keeper.

1772   Publishes his first pamphlet, *The Case of the Officers of Excise,* a plea for higher salaries for revenue officers.

1774   Dismissed from the excise service for leaving his post without permission; separates from his wife and sells their household possessions at public auction; sails across the Atlantic to Philadelphia, Pennsylvania.

January 1775   Becomes the editor of the *Pennsylvania Magazine,* to which he contributes anonymous essays and poems; becomes an avid supporter of American independence against British rule.

December 1775   Completes the writing of *Common Sense.*

1776–1777   Serves in the Patriot forces, initially as the secretary to General Daniel Roberdeau and subsequently as an aide-de-camp to General Nathanael Greene.

January 1776   Publishes *Common Sense* to promote American independence, a union of the states, and a republican government.

4 July 1776   The Continental Congress announces its Declaration of Independence.

December 1776   Publishes the first installment of *The American Crisis,* a collection of essays to revive the morale of the Patriots at a low ebb in their military struggle against the British forces. From 1777 to 1783, he would publish twelve more essays in this series to offer his views on the war and politics.

1778   Becomes secretary to the Committee on Foreign Affairs of Congress; publishes essays accusing Silas Deane, a congressional envoy to France, of corruption. Congress forces Paine to resign as secretary for having cited secret diplomatic correspondence.

1779   Serves on an extralegal committee to restrain inflation by setting prices, an effort which soon collapses.

1782   Publishes essays to promote a stronger national government with the power to levy taxes on imports.

1786   Publishes *Dissertations on Government, the Affairs of the Bank, and Paper Money* to promote Robert Morris's Bank of North America; Congress pays Paine $3,000 for his services during the war, and the New York state legislature grants him the confiscated property of a Loyalist in New Rochelle.

1787   The Pennsylvania legislature rejects his bid to secure funding for an experimental wrought-iron bridge, so Paine embarks for France, and later Britain, to seek investors (also in vain).

1791–1792   Publishes in London (in two installments) *The Rights of Man* to vindicate the republican revolution in France from the conservative critique published the year before by Edmund Burke. Indicted by the government for sedition, Paine flees the country.

September 1792   Finding haven in France, Paine wins election to the National Convention, where he votes to abolish the monarchy but opposes the execution of the king and queen.

December 1793   Associated with the Girondin moderates, Paine suffers arrest at the hands of their triumphant, and more radical, rivals, the Jacobins.

November 1794   Released from prison in Paris, publishes *The Age of Reason,* a deist attack on institutionalized Christianity and on Christian fundamentalism.

1795–1796   Publishes two controversial letters denouncing the American president, George Washington, as a treacherous hypocrite for doing too little to secure Paine's early release from prison.

1797   Publishes *Agrarian Justice* to promote land reform to benefit the poor.

1802   At the invitation of the new American president, Thomas Jefferson, Paine leaves France to return to the United States. He settles on his farm in New Rochelle, New York, and publishes magazine essays promoting deism.

1808   Moves to Greenwich Village in New York City, where he lives in obscurity and poverty.

9 June 1809   Dies at age seventy-two without children.

1819   The British journalist and reformer William Cobbett disinters Paine's remains and takes them to England for reburial in a projected monument. Nothing came of that project, and Paine's bones became lost after Cobbett's death.

COMMON SENSE

ADDRESSED TO THE INHABITANTS OF AMERICA

Man knows no Master save creating HEAVEN,
Or those whom Choice and common Good ordain.

Thomson

Introduction

PERHAPS THE SENTIMENTS contained in the following pages, are not *yet* sufficiently fashionable to procure them general favor; a long habit of not thinking a thing *wrong*, gives it a superficial appearance of being *right*, and raises at first a formidable outcry in defence of custom. But the tumult soon subsides. Time makes more converts than reason.

As a long and violent abuse of power, is generally the Means of calling the right of it in question (and in Matters too which might never have been thought of, had not the Sufferers been aggravated into the inquiry) and as the King of England hath undertaken in his *own Right,* to support the Parliament in what he calls *Theirs,* and as the good people of this country are grievously oppressed by the combination, they have an undoubted privilege to inquire into the pretensions of both, and equally to reject the usurpation of either.

In the following sheets, the author hath studiously avoided every thing which is personal among ourselves. Compliments as well as censure to individuals make no part thereof. The wise, and the worthy, need not the triumph of a pamphlet; and those whose sentiments are injudicious, or unfriendly, will cease of themselves unless too much pains are bestowed upon their conversion.

The cause of America is in a great measure the cause of all mankind. Many circumstances hath, and will arise, which are not local, but universal, and through which the principles of all Lovers of Mankind are affected, and in the Event of which, their Affections are interested. The laying a Country desolate with Fire and Sword, declaring War against the natural rights of all Mankind, and extirpating the Defenders thereof from the Face of the Earth, is the Concern of every Man to whom Nature hath given the Power of feeling; of which Class, regardless of Party Censure, is the

AUTHOR.

P.S. The Publication of this new Edition hath been delayed, with a View of taking notice (had it been necessary) of any Attempt to refute the Doctrine of Independance: As no Answer hath yet appeared, it is now presumed that none will, the Time needful for getting such a Performance ready for the Public being considerably past.

Who the Author of this Production is, is wholly unnecessary to the Public, as the Object for Attention is the *Doctrine itself,* not the *Man.* Yet it may not be unnecessary to say, That he is unconnected with any Party, and under no sort of Influence public or private, but the influence of reason and principle.

Philadelphia, February 14, 1776.

COMMON SENSE

Of the Origin and Design of Government in General. With Concise Remarks on the English Constitution.

SOME writers have so confounded society with government, as to leave little or no distinction between them; whereas they are not only different, but have different origins. Society is produced by our wants, and government by our wickedness; the former promotes our happiness *positively* by uniting our affections, the latter *negatively* by restraining our vices. The one encourages intercourse, the other creates distinctions. The first is a patron, the last a punisher.

Society in every state is a blessing, but government even in its best state is but a necessary evil; in its worst state an intolerable one; for when we suffer, or are exposed to the same miseries *by a government*, which we might expect in a country *without government*, our calamity is heightened by reflecting that we furnish the means by which we suffer. Government, like dress, is the badge of lost innocence; the palaces of kings are built on the ruins of the bowers of paradise. For were the impulses of conscience clear, uniform, and irresistably obeyed, man would need no other lawgiver; but that not being the case, he finds it necessary to surrender up a part of his property to furnish means for the protection of the rest; and this he is induced to do by the same prudence which in every other case advises him out of two evils to choose the least. *Wherefore*, security being the true design and end of government, it unanswerably follows that whatever *form* thereof appears most likely to ensure it to us, with the least expense and greatest benefit, is preferable to all others.

In order to gain a clear and just idea of the design and end of government, let us suppose a small number of persons settled in some sequestered part of the earth, unconnected with the rest, they will then represent the first peopling of any country, or of the world. In this state of natural liberty, society will be their first thought. A thousand motives will excite them thereto, the strength of one man is so unequal to his wants, and his mind so unfitted for perpetual solitude, that he is soon obliged to seek assistance and relief of another, who in his turn requires the same. Four or five united would be able to raise a tolerable dwelling in the midst of a wilderness, but *one* man might labour out the common period of life without accomplishing any thing; when he had felled his timber he could not remove it, nor erect it after it was removed; hunger in the mean time would urge him from his work, and every different want call him a different way. Disease, nay even misfortune would be death, for though neither might be mortal, yet either would disable him from living, and reduce him to a state in which he might rather be said to perish than to die.

Thus necessity, like a gravitating power, would soon form our newly arrived emigrants into society, the reciprocal blessings of which, would supersede, and render the obligations of law and government unnecessary while they remained perfectly just to each other; but as nothing but heaven is impregnable to vice, it will unavoidably happen, that in proportion as they surmount the first difficulties of emigration, which bound them together in a common cause, they will begin to relax in their duty and attachment to each other; and this remissness, will point out the necessity, of establishing some form of government to supply the defect of moral virtue.

Some convenient tree will afford them a State-House, under the branches of which, the whole colony may assemble to deliberate on public matters. It is more than probable that their first laws will have the title only of REGULATIONS, and be enforced by no other penalty than public disesteem. In this first parliament every man, by natural right, will have a seat.

But as the colony increases, the public concerns will increase likewise, and the distance at which the members may be separated, will render it too inconvenient for all of them to meet on every occasion as at first, when their number was small, their habitations near, and the public concerns few and trifling. This will point out the convenience of their consenting to leave the legislative part to be managed by a select number chosen from the whole body, who are supposed to have the same concerns at stake which those have who appointed them, and who will act in the same manner as the whole body would act were they present. If the colony continue increasing, it will become necessary to augment the number of the representatives, and that the interest of every part of the colony may be attended to, it will be found best to divide the whole into convenient parts, each part sending its proper number; and that the *elected* might never form to themselves an interest separate from the *electors,* prudence will point out the propriety of having elections often; because as the *elected* might by that means return and mix again with the general body of the *electors* in a few months, their fidelity to the public will be secured by the prudent reflexion of not making a rod for themselves. And as this frequent interchange will establish a common interest with every part of the community, they will mutually and naturally support each other, and on this (not on the unmeaning name of king) depends the *strength of government, and the happiness of the governed.*

Here then is the origin and rise of government; namely, a mode rendered necessary by the inability of moral virtue to govern the world; here too is the design and end of government, viz. freedom and security. And however our eyes may be dazzled with show, or our ears deceived by sound; however prejudice may warp our wills, or interest darken our understanding, the simple voice of nature and of reason will say, it is right.

I draw my idea of the form of government from a principle in nature, which no art can overturn, viz. that the more simple any thing is, the less liable it is to be disordered, and the easier repaired when disordered; and with this maxim in view, I offer a few remarks on the so much boasted constitution of England. That it was noble for the dark and slavish times in which it was erected, is granted. When the world was over run with tyranny the least remove therefrom was a glorious rescue. But that it is imperfect, subject to convulsions, and incapable of producing what it seems to promise, is easily demonstrated.

Absolute governments (tho' the disgrace of human nature) have this advantage with them, that they are simple; if the people suffer, they know the head from which their suffering springs, know likewise the remedy, and are not bewildered by a variety of causes and cures. But the constitution of England is so exceedingly complex, that the nation may suffer for years together without being able to discover in which part the fault lies, some will say in one and some in another, and every political physician will advise a different medicine.

I know it is difficult to get over local or long standing prejudices, yet if we will suffer ourselves to examine the component parts of the English constitution, we shall find them to be the base remains of two ancient tyrannies, compounded with some new republican materials.

First.—The remains of monarchical tyranny in the person of the king.

Secondly.—The remains of aristocratical tyranny in the persons of the peers.

Thirdly.—The new republican materials, in the persons of the commons, on whose virtue depends the freedom of England.

The two first, by being hereditary, are independent of the people; wherefore in a *constitutional sense* they contribute nothing towards the freedom of the state.

To say that the constitution of England is a *union* of three powers reciprocally *checking* each other, is farcical, either the words have no meaning, or they are flat contradictions.

To say that the commons is a check upon the king, presupposes two things.

First.—That the king is not to be trusted without being looked after, or in other words, that a thirst for absolute power is the natural disease of monarchy.

Secondly.—That the commons, by being appointed for that purpose, are either wiser or more worthy of confidence than the crown.

But as the same constitution which gives the commons a power to check the king by withholding the supplies, gives afterwards the king a power to check the commons, by empowering him to reject their other bills; it again supposes that the king is wiser than those whom it has already supposed to be wiser than him. A mere absurdity!

There is something exceedingly ridiculous in the composition of monarchy; it first excludes a man from the means of information, yet empowers him to act in cases where the highest judgment is required. The state of a king shuts him from the world, yet the business of a king requires him to know it thoroughly; wherefore the different parts, by unnaturally opposing and destroying each other, prove the whole character to be absurd and useless.

Some writers have explained the English constitution thus; the king, say they, is one, the people another; the peers are an house in behalf of the king; the commons in behalf of the people; but this hath all the distinctions of an house divided against itself; and though the expressions be pleasantly arranged, yet when examined they appear idle and ambiguous; and it will always happen, that the nicest construction that words are capable of, when applied to the description of some thing which either cannot exist, or is too incomprehensible to be within the compass of description, will be words of sound only, and though they may amuse the ear, they cannot inform the mind, for this explanation includes a previous question, viz. *How came the king by a power which the people are afraid to trust, and always obliged to check?* Such a power could not be the gift of a wise people, neither can any power, *which needs checking,* be from God; yet the provision, which the constitution makes, supposes such a power to exist.

But the provision is unequal to the task; the means either cannot or will not accomplish the end, and the whole affair is a felo de se; for as the greater weight will always carry up the less, and as all the wheels of a machine are put in motion by one, it only remains to know which power in the constitution has the most weight, for that will govern; and though the others, or a part of them, may clog, or, as the phrase is, check the rapidity of its motion, yet so long as they cannot stop it, their endeavors will be ineffectual; the first moving power will at last have its way, and what it wants in speed is supplied by time.

That the crown is this overbearing part in the English constitution needs not be mentioned, and that it derives its whole consequence merely from being the giver of places and pensions is self-evident, wherefore, though we have been wise enough to shut and lock a door against absolute monarchy, we at the same time have been foolish enough to put the crown in possession of the key.

The prejudice of Englishmen, in favour of their own government by king, lords and commons, arises as much or more from national pride than reason. Individuals are undoubtedly safer in England than in some other countries, but the *will* of the king is as much the *law* of the land in Britain as in France, with this difference, that instead of proceeding directly from his mouth, it is handed to the people under the most formidable shape of an act of parliament. For the fate of Charles the First, hath only made kings more subtle—not more just.

Wherefore, laying aside all national pride and prejudice in favour of modes and forms, the plain truth is, that *it is wholly owing to the constitution of the people, and not to the constitution of the government* that the crown is not as oppressive in England as in Turkey.

An inquiry into the *constitutional errors* in the English form of government is at this time highly necessary; for as we are never in a proper condition of doing justice to others, while we continue under the influence of some leading partiality, so neither are we capable of doing it to ourselves while we remain fettered by any obstinate prejudice. And as a man, who is attached to a prostitute, is unfitted to choose or judge of a wife, so any prepossession in favour of a rotten constitution of government will disable us from discerning a good one.

Of Monarchy and Hereditary Succession.

MANKIND being originally equals in the order of creation, the equality could only be destroyed by some subsequent circumstance; the distinctions of rich, and poor, may in a great measure be accounted for, and that without having recourse to the harsh ill sounding names of oppression and avarice. Oppression is often the *consequence*, but seldom or never the *means* of riches; and though avarice will preserve a man from being necessitously poor, it generally makes him too timorous to be wealthy.

But there is another and greater distinction for which no truly natural or religious reason can be assigned, and that is, the distinction of men into KINGS and SUBJECTS. Male and female are the distinctions of nature, good and bad the distinctions of heaven; but how a race of men came into the world so exalted above the rest, and distinguished like some new species, is worth enquiring into, and whether they are the means of happiness or of misery to mankind.

In the early ages of the world, according to the scripture chronology, there were no kings; the consequence of which was there were no wars; it is the pride of kings which throw mankind into confusion. Holland without a king hath enjoyed more peace for this last century than any of the monarchical governments in Europe. Antiquity favors the same remark; for the quiet and rural lives of the first patriarchs hath a happy something in them, which vanishes away when we come to the history of Jewish royalty.

Government by kings was first introduced into the world by the Heathens, from whom the children of Israel copied the custom. It was the most prosperous invention the Devil ever set on foot for the promotion of idolatry. The Heathens paid divine honors to their deceased kings, and the christian world hath improved on the plan by doing the same to their living ones. How impious is the title of sacred majesty applied to a worm, who in the midst of his splendor is crumbling into dust!

As the exalting one man so greatly above the rest cannot be justified on the equal rights of nature, so neither can it be defended on the authority of scripture; for the will of the Almighty, as declared by Gideon and the prophet Samuel, expressly disapproves of government by kings. All anti-monarchical parts of scripture have been very smoothly glossed over in monarchical governments, but they undoubtedly merit the attention of countries which have their governments yet to form. *"Render unto Cæsar the things which are Cæsar's"* is the scriptural doctrine of courts, yet it is no support of monarchical government, for the Jews at that time were without a king, and in a state of vassalage to the Romans.

Near three thousand years passed away from the Mosaic account of the creation, till the Jews under a national delusion requested a king. Till then their form of government (except in extraordinary cases, where the Almighty interposed) was a kind of republic administered by a judge and the elders of the tribes. Kings they had none, and it was held sinful to acknowledge any being under that title but the Lord of Hosts. And when a man seriously reflects on the idolatrous homage which is paid to the persons of Kings, he need not wonder, that the Almighty ever jealous of his honor, should disapprove of a form of government which so impiously invades the prerogative of heaven.

Monarchy is ranked in scripture as one of the sins of the Jews, for which a curse in reserve is denounced against them. The history of that transaction is worth attending to.

The children of Israel being oppressed by the Midianites, Gideon marched against them with a small army, and victory, thro' the divine interposition, decided in his favour. The Jews elate with success, and attributing it to the generalship of Gideon, proposed making him a king, saying, *Rule thou over us, thou and thy son and thy son's son.* Here was temptation in its fullest extent; not a kingdom only, but an hereditary one, but Gideon in the piety of his soul replied, *I will not rule over you, neither shall my son rule over you,* THE LORD SHALL RULE OVER YOU. Words need not be more explicit; Gideon doth not *decline* the honor, but denieth their right to give it; neither doth he compliment them with invented declarations of his thanks, but in the positive stile of a prophet charges them with disaffection to their proper Sovereign, the King of heaven.

About one hundred and thirty years after this, they fell again into the same error. The hankering which the Jews had for the idolatrous customs of the Heathens, is something exceedingly unaccountable; but so it was, that laying hold of the misconduct of Samuel's two sons, who were entrusted with some secular concerns, they came in an abrupt and clamorous manner to Samuel, saying, *Behold thou art old, and thy sons walk not in thy ways, now make us a king to judge us like all the other nations.* And here we cannot but observe that their motives were bad, viz. that they might be *like* unto other nations, i.e. the Heathens, whereas their true glory laid in being as much *unlike* them as possible. *But the thing displeased Samuel when they said, Give us a king to judge us; and Samuel prayed unto the Lord, and the Lord said unto Samuel, Hearken unto the voice of the people in all that they say unto thee, for they have not rejected thee, but they have rejected me,* THAT I SHOULD NOT REIGN OVER THEM. *According to all the works which they have done since the day that I brought them up out of Egypt, even unto this day; wherewith they have forsaken me and served other Gods; so do they also unto thee. Now therefore hearken unto their voice, howbeit, protest solemnly unto them and shew them the manner of the king that shall reign over them,* i. e. not of any particular king, but the general manner of the kings of the earth, whom Israel was so eagerly copying after. And notwithstanding the great distance of time and difference of manners, the character is still in fashion. *And Samuel told all the words of the Lord unto the people, that asked of him a king. And he said, This shall be the manner of the king that shall reign over you; he will take your sons and appoint them for himself, for his chariots, and to be his horsemen, and some shall run before his chariots* (this description agrees with the present mode of impressing men) *and he will appoint him captains over thousands and captains over fifties, and will set them to ear his ground and to reap his harvest, and to make his instruments of war, and instruments of his chariots; and he will take your daughters to be confectionaries, and to be cooks and to be bakers* (this describes the expence and luxury as well as the oppression of kings) *and he will take your fields and your olive yards, even the best of them, and give them to his servants; and he will take the tenth of your seed, and of your vineyards, and give them to his officers and to his servants* (by which we see that bribery, corruption and favoritism are the standing vices of kings) *and he will take the tenth of your men servants, and your maid servants, and your goodliest young men and your asses, and put them to his work; and he will take the tenth of your sheep, and ye shall be his servants, and ye shall cry out in that day because of your king which ye shall have chosen,* AND THE LORD WILL NOT HEAR YOU IN THAT DAY. This accounts for the continuation of monarchy; neither do the characters of the few good kings which have lived since, either sanctify the title, or blot out the sinfulness of the origin; the high encomium given of David takes no notice of him *officially as a king,* but only as a *man* after God's own heart. *Nevertheless the People refused to obey the voice of Samuel, and they said, Nay, but we will have a king over us, that we may be like all the nations, and that our king may judge us, and go out before us, and fight our battles.* Samuel continued to reason with them, but to no purpose; he set before them their ingratitude, but all would not avail; and seeing them fully bent on their folly, he cried out, *I will call unto the Lord, and he shall send thunder and rain* (which then was a punishment, being in the time of wheat harvest) *that ye may perceive and see that your wickedness is great which ye have done in the sight of the Lord,* IN ASKING YOU A KING. *So Samuel called unto the Lord, and the Lord sent thunder and rain that day, and all the people greatly feared the Lord and Samuel. And all the people said unto Samuel, Pray for thy servants unto the Lord thy God that we die not, for* WE HAVE ADDED UNTO OUR SINS THIS EVIL, TO ASK A KING. These portions of scripture are direct and positive. They admit of no equivocal construction. That the Almighty hath here entered his protest against monarchical government is true, or the scripture is false. And a man hath good reason to believe that there is as much of king-craft, as priest-craft, in withholding the scripture from the public in Popish countries. For monarchy in every instance is the Popery of government.

To the evil of monarchy we have added that of hereditary succession; and as the first is a degradation and lessening of ourselves, so the second, claimed as a matter of right, is an insult and an imposition on posterity. For all men being originally equals, no *one* by *birth* could have a right to set up his own family in perpetual preference to all others for ever, and though himself might deserve *some* decent degree of honors of his cotemporaries, yet his descendants might be far too unworthy to inherit them. One of the strongest *natural* proofs of the folly of hereditary right in kings, is, that nature disapproves it, otherwise she would not so frequently turn it into ridicule by giving mankind an *ass for a lion.*

Secondly, as no man at first could possess any other public honors than were bestowed upon him, so the givers of those honors could have no power to give away the right of posterity, and though they might say, "We choose you for *our* head," they could not, without manifest injustice to their children, say "that your children and your childrens children shall reign over *ours* for ever." Because such an unwise, unjust, unnatural compact might (perhaps) in the next succession put them under the government of a rogue or a fool. Most wise men, in their private sentiments, have ever treated hereditary right with contempt; yet it is one of those evils, which when once established is not easily removed; many submit from fear, others from superstition, and the more powerful part shares with the king the plunder of the rest.

This is supposing the present race of kings in the world to have had an honorable origin; whereas it is more than probable, that could we take off the dark covering of antiquity, and trace them to their first rise, that we should find the first of them nothing better than the principal ruffian of some restless gang, whose savage manners of preeminence in subtility obtained him the title of chief among plunderers; and who by increasing in power, and extending his depredations, over-awed the quiet and defenseless to purchase their safety by frequent contributions. Yet his electors could have no idea of giving hereditary right to his descendants, because such a perpetual exclusion of themselves was incompatible with the free and unrestrained principles they professed to live by. Wherefore, hereditary succession in the early ages of monarchy could not take place as a matter of claim, but as something casual or complimental; but as few or no records were extant in those days, and traditionary history stuffed with fables, it was very easy, after the lapse of a few generations, to trump up some superstitious tale, conveniently timed, Mahomet like, to cram hereditary right down the throats of the vulgar. Perhaps the disorders which threatened, or seemed to threaten, on the decease of a leader and the choice of a new one (for elections among ruffians could not be very orderly) induced many at first to favor hereditary pretensions; by which means it happened, as it hath happened since, that what at first was submitted to as a convenience, was afterwards claimed as a right.

England, since the conquest, hath known some few good monarchs, but groaned beneath a much larger number of bad ones; yet no man in his senses can say that their claim under William the Conqueror is a very honorable one. A French bastard landing with an armed banditti, and establishing himself king of England against the consent of the natives, is in plain terms a very paltry rascally original. —It certainly hath no divinity in it. However, it is needless to spend much time in exposing the folly of hereditary right, if there are any so weak as to believe it, let them promiscuously worship the ass and lion, and welcome. I shall neither copy their humility, nor disturb their devotion.

Yet I should be glad to ask how they suppose kings came at first? The question admits but of three answers, viz. either by lot, by election, or by usurpation. If the first king was taken by lot, it establishes a precedent for the next, which excludes hereditary succession. Saul was by lot, yet the succession was not hereditary, neither does it appear from that transaction there was any intention it ever should. If the first king of any country was by election, that likewise establishes

a precedent for the next; for to say, that the *right* of all future generations is taken away, by the act of the first electors, in their choice not
only of a king, but of a family of kings for ever, hath no parrallel in or
out of scripture but the doctrine of original sin, which supposes the
free will of all men lost in Adam; and from such comparison, and it
will admit of no other, hereditary succession can derive no glory. For
as in Adam all sinned, and as in the first electors all men obeyed; as in
the one all mankind were subjected to Satan, and in the other to Sovereignty; as our innocence was lost in the first, and our authority in
the last; and as both disable us from reassuming some former state
and privilege, it unanswerably follows that original sin and hereditary succession are parallels. Dishonorable rank! Inglorious connexion! Yet the most subtile sophist cannot produce a juster simile.

As to usurpation, no man will be so hardy as to defend it; and that
William the Conqueror was an usurper is a fact not to be contra-
dicted. The plain truth is, that the antiquity of English monarchy will
not bear looking into.

But it is not so much the absurdity as the evil of hereditary succession which concerns mankind. Did it ensure a race of good and wise
men it would have the seal of divine authority, but as it opens a door
to the *foolish,* the *wicked,* and the *improper,* it hath in it the nature of
oppression. Men who look upon themselves born to reign, and others
to obey, soon grow insolent; selected from the rest of mankind their
minds are early poisoned by importance; and the world they act in
differs so materially from the world at large, that they have but little opportunity of knowing its true interests, and when they succeed
to the government are frequently the most ignorant and unfit of any
throughout the dominions.

Another evil which attends hereditary succession is, that the
throne is subject to be possessed by a minor at any age; all which time
the regency, acting under the cover of a king, have every opportunity
and inducement to betray their trust. The same national misfortune

happens, when a king worn out with age and infirmity, enters the last stage of human weakness. In both these cases the public becomes a prey to every miscreant, who can tamper successfully with the follies either of age or infancy.

The most plausible plea, which hath ever been offered in favour of hereditary succession, is, that it preserves a nation from civil wars; and were this true, it would be weighty; whereas, it is the most barefaced falsity ever imposed upon mankind. The whole history of England disowns the fact. Thirty kings and two minors have reigned in that distracted kingdom since the conquest, in which time there have been (including the Revolution) no less than eight civil wars and nineteen rebellions. Wherefore instead of making for peace, it makes against it, and destroys the very foundation it seems to stand on.

The contest for monarchy and succession, between the houses of York and Lancaster, laid England in a scene of blood for many years. Twelve pitched battles, besides skirmishes and sieges, were fought between Henry and Edward. Twice was Henry prisoner to Edward, who in his turn was prisoner to Henry. And so uncertain is the fate of war and the temper of a nation, when nothing but personal matters are the ground of a quarrel, that Henry was taken in triumph from a prison to a palace, and Edward obliged to fly from a palace to a foreign land; yet, as sudden transitions of temper are seldom lasting, Henry in his turn was driven from the throne, and Edward recalled to succeed him. The parliament always following the strongest side.

This contest began in the reign of Henry the Sixth, and was not entirely extinguished till Henry the Seventh, in whom the families were united. Including a period of 67 years, viz. from 1422 to 1489.

In short, monarchy and succession have laid (not this or that kingdom only) but the world in blood and ashes. 'Tis a form of government which the word of God bears testimony against, and blood will attend it.

If we inquire into the business of a king, we shall find that in some countries they have none; and after sauntering away their lives without pleasure to themselves or advantage to the nation, withdraw from the scene, and leave their successors to tread the same idle round. In absolute monarchies the whole weight of business, civil and military, lies on the king; the children of Israel in their request for a king, urged this plea "that he may judge us, and go out before us and fight our battles." But in countries where he is neither a judge nor a general, as in England, a man would be puzzled to know what *is* his business.

The nearer any government approaches to a republic the less business there is for a king. It is somewhat difficult to find a proper name for the government of England. Sir William Meredith calls it a republic; but in its present state it is unworthy of the name, because the corrupt influence of the crown, by having all the places in its disposal, hath so effectually swallowed up the power, and eaten out the virtue of the house of commons (the republican part in the constitution) that the government of England is nearly as monarchical as that of France or Spain. Men fall out with names without understanding them. For it is the republican and not the monarchical part of the constitution of England which Englishmen glory in, viz. the liberty of choosing an house of commons from out of their own body—and it is easy to see that when republican virtue fails, slavery ensues. Why is the constitution of England sickly, but because monarchy hath poisoned the republic, the crown hath engrossed the commons?

In England a king hath little more to do than to make war and give away places; which in plain terms, is to impoverish the nation and set it together by the ears. A pretty business indeed for a man to be allowed eight hundred thousand sterling a year for, and worshipped into the bargain! Of more worth is one honest man to society, and in the sight of God, than all the crowned ruffians that ever lived.

Thoughts of the Present State
of American Affairs.

I N the following pages I offer nothing more than simple facts, plain arguments, and common sense; and have no other preliminaries to settle with the reader, than that he will divest himself of prejudice and prepossession, and suffer his reason and his feelings to determine for themselves; that he will put *on*, or rather that he will not put *off*, the true character of a man, and generously enlarge his views beyond the present day.

Volumes have been written on the subject of the struggle between England and America. Men of all ranks have embarked in the controversy, from different motives, and with various designs; but all have been ineffectual, and the period of debate is closed. Arms, as the last resource, decide the contest; the appeal was the choice of the king, and the continent hath accepted the challenge.

It hath been reported of the late Mr. Pelham (who tho' an able minister was not without his faults) that on his being attacked in the house of commons, on the score, that his measures were only of a temporary kind, replied "*they will last my time.*" Should a thought so fatal and unmanly possess the colonies in the present contest, the name of ancestors will be remembered by future generations with detestation.

The sun never shined on a cause of greater worth. 'Tis not the affair of a city, a county, a province, or a kingdom, but of a continent— of at least one eighth part of the habitable globe. 'Tis not the concern of a day, a year, or an age; posterity are virtually involved in the contest, and will be more or less affected, even to the end of time, by the proceedings now. Now is the seed time of continental union, faith and honor. The least fracture now will be like a name engraved with the point of a pin on the tender rind of a young oak; the wound will enlarge with the tree, and posterity read it in full grown characters.

By referring the matter from argument to arms, a new æra for politics is struck; a new method of thinking hath arisen. All plans, proposals, &c. prior to the nineteenth of April, *i. e.* to the commencement of hostilities, are like the almanacks of the last year; which, though proper then, are superceded and useless now. Whatever was advanced by the advocates on either side of the question then, terminated in one and the same point, viz. a union with Great-Britain; the only difference between the parties was the method of effecting it; the one proposing force, the other friendship; but it hath so far happened that the first hath failed, and the second hath withdrawn her influence.

As much hath been said of the advantages of reconciliation, which, like an agreeable dream, hath passed away and left us as we were, it is but right, that we should examine the contrary side of the argument, and inquire into some of the many material injuries which these colonies sustain, and always will sustain, by being connected with, and dependant on Great-Britain. To examine that connexion and dependance, on the principles of nature and common sense, to see what we have to trust to, if separated, and what we are to expect, if dependant.

I have heard it asserted by some, that as America hath flourished under her former connexion with Great-Britain, that the same connexion is necessary towards her future happiness, and will always have the same effect. Nothing can be more fallacious than this kind of argument. We may as well assert that because a child has thrived upon milk, that it is never to have meat, or that the first twenty years of our lives is to become a precedent for the next twenty. But even this is admitting more than is true, for I answer roundly, that America would have flourished as much, and probably much more, had no European power had any thing to do with her. The commerce, by which she hath enriched herself are the necessaries of life, and will always have a market while eating is the custom of Europe.

But she has protected us, say some. That she hath engrossed us is true, and defended the continent at our expence as well as her own is admitted, and she would have defended Turkey from the same motive, viz. the sake of trade and dominion.

Alas, we have been long led away by ancient prejudices, and made large sacrifices to superstition. We have boasted the protection of Great-Britain, without considering, that her motive was *interest* not *attachment;* that she did not protect us from *our enemies* on *our account,* but from *her enemies* on *her own account,* from those who had no quarrel with us on any *other account,* and who will always be our enemies on the *same account.* Let Britain wave her pretensions to the continent, or the continent throw off the dependance, and we should be at peace with France and Spain were they at war with Britain. The miseries of Hanover last war ought to warn us against connexions.

It hath lately been asserted in parliament, that the colonies have no relation to each other but through the parent country, *i. e.* that Pennsylvania and the Jerseys, and so on for the rest, are sister colonies by the way of England; this is certainly a very round-about way of proving relationship, but it is the nearest and only true way of proving enemyship, if I may so call it. France and Spain never were, nor perhaps ever will be our enemies as *Americans*, but as our being the *subjects of Great-Britain.*

But Britain is the parent country, say some. Then the more shame upon her conduct. Even brutes do not devour their young, nor savages make war upon their families; wherefore the assertion, if true, turns to her reproach; but it happens not to be true, or only partly so, and the phrase *parent* or *mother country* hath been jesuitically adopted by the king and his parasites, with a low papistical design of gaining an unfair bias on the credulous weakness of our minds. Europe, and not England, is the parent country of America. This new world hath been the asylum for the persecuted lovers of civil and religious liberty from *every part* of Europe. Hither have they fled, not from the tender embraces of the mother, but from the cruelty of the monster; and it is so far true of England, that the same tyranny which drove the first emigrants from home, pursues their descendants still.

In this extensive quarter of the globe, we forget the narrow limits of three hundred and sixty miles (the extent of England) and carry our friendship on a larger scale; we claim brotherhood with every European christian, and triumph in the generosity of the sentiment.

It is pleasant to observe by what regular gradations we surmount the force of local prejudice, as we enlarge our acquaintance with the world. A man born in any town in England divided into parishes, will naturally associate most with his fellow parishioners (because their interests in many cases will be common) and distinguish him by the name of *neighbour;* if he meet him but a few miles from home, he drops the narrow idea of a street, and salutes him by the name of *townsman;* if he travels out of the county, and meet him in any other, he forgets the minor divisions of street and town, and calls him *countryman,* i. e. *county-man;* but if in their foreign excursions they should associate in France or any other part of *Europe,* their local remembrance would be enlarged into that of *Englishmen.* And by a just parity of reasoning, all Europeans meeting in America, or any other quarter of the globe, are *countrymen*; for England, Holland, Germany, or Sweden, when compared with the whole, stand in the same places on the larger scale, which the divisions of street, town, and county do on the smaller ones; distinctions too limited for continental minds. Not one third of the inhabitants, even of this province, are of English descent. Wherefore I reprobate the phrase of parent or mother country applied to England only, as being false, selfish, narrow and ungenerous.

But admitting, that we were all of English descent, what does it amount to? Nothing. Britain, being now an open enemy, extinguishes every other name and title: And to say that reconciliation is our duty, is truly farcical. The first king of England, of the present line (William the Conqueror) was a Frenchman, and half the Peers of England are descendants from the same country; wherefore, by the same method of reasoning, England ought to be governed by France.

Much hath been said of the united strength of Britain and the colonies, that in conjunction they might bid defiance to the world. But this is mere presumption; the fate of war is uncertain, neither do the expressions mean any thing; for this continent would never suffer itself to be drained of inhabitants, to support the British arms in either Asia, Africa, or Europe.

Besides, what have we to do with setting the world at defiance? Our plan is commerce, and that, well attended to, will secure us the peace and friendship of all Europe; because, it is the interest of all Europe to have America a *free port*. Her trade will always be a protection, and her barrenness of gold and silver secure her from invaders.

I challenge the warmest advocate for reconciliation, to shew, a single advantage that this continent can reap, by being connected with Great Britain. I repeat the challenge, not a single advantage is derived. Our corn will fetch its price in any market in Europe, and our imported goods must be paid for buy them where we will.

But the injuries and disadvantages we sustain by that connection, are without number; and our duty to mankind at large, as well as to ourselves, instruct us to renounce the alliance: Because, any submission to, or dependance on Great-Britain, tends directly to involve this continent in European wars and quarrels; and sets us at variance with nations, who would otherwise seek our friendship, and against whom, we have neither anger nor complaint. As Europe is our market for trade, we ought to form no partial connection with any part of it. It is the true interest of America to steer clear of European contentions, which she never can do, while by her dependance on Britain, she is made the make-weight in the scale of British politics.

Europe is too thickly planted with kingdoms to be long at peace, and whenever a war breaks out between England and any foreign power, the trade of America goes to ruin, *because of her connection with Britain.* The next war may not turn out like the last, and should it not, the advocates for reconciliation now will be wishing for separation then, because, neutrality in that case, would be a safer convoy than a man of war. Every thing that is right or natural pleads for separation. The blood of the slain, the weeping voice of nature cries, 'Tis TIME TO PART. Even the distance at which the Almighty hath placed England and America, is a strong and natural proof, that the authority of the one, over the other, was never the design of Heaven. The time likewise at which the continent was discovered, adds weight to the argument, and the manner in which it was peopled encreases the force of it. The reformation was preceded by the discovery of America, as if the Almighty graciously meant to open a sanctuary to the persecuted in future years, when home should afford neither friendship nor safety.

The authority of Great-Britain over this continent, is a form of government, which sooner or later must have an end: And a serious mind can draw no true pleasure by looking forward, under the painful and positive conviction, that what he calls "the present constitution" is merely temporary. As parents, we can have no joy, knowing that *this government* is not sufficiently lasting to ensure any thing which we may bequeath to posterity: And by a plain method of argument, as we are running the next generation into debt, we ought to do the work of it, otherwise we use them meanly and pitifully. In order to discover the line of our duty rightly, we should take our children in our hand, and fix our station a few years farther into life; that eminence will present a prospect, which a few present fears and prejudices conceal from our sight.

Though I would carefully avoid giving unnecessary offence, yet I am inclined to believe, that all those who espouse the doctrine of reconciliation, may be included within the following descriptions: Interested men, who are not to be trusted; weak men who *cannot* see; prejudiced men who *will not* see; and a certain set of moderate men, who think better of the European world than it deserves; and this last class, by an ill-judged deliberation, will be the cause of more calamities to this continent, than all the other three.

It is the good fortune of many to live distant from the scene of sorrow; the evil is not sufficiently brought to *their* doors to make *them* feel the precariousness with which all American property is possessed. But let our imaginations transport us for a few moments to Boston, that seat of wretchedness will teach us wisdom, and instruct us for ever to renounce a power in whom we can have no trust. The inhabitants of that unfortunate city, who but a few months ago were in ease and affluence, have now, no other alternative than to stay and starve, or turn out to beg. Endangered by the fire of their friends if they continue within the city, and plundered by the soldiery if they leave it. In their present condition they are prisoners without the hope of redemption, and in a general attack for their relief, they would be exposed to the fury of both armies.

Men of passive tempers look somewhat lightly over the offences of Britain, and, still hoping for the best, are apt to call out, *"Come, come, we shall be friends again, for all this."* But examine the passions and feelings of mankind, Bring the doctrine of reconciliation to the touchstone of nature, and then tell me, whether you can hereafter love, honour, and faithfully serve the power that hath carried fire and sword into your land? If you cannot do all these, then are you only deceiving yourselves, and by your delay bringing ruin upon posterity. Your future connection with Britain, whom you can neither love nor honour, will be forced and unnatural, and being formed only on the plan of present convenience, will in a little time fall into a relapse more wretched than the first. But if you say, you can still pass the violations over, then I ask, Hath your house been burnt? Hath your property been destroyed before your face? Are your wife and children destitute of a bed to lie on, or bread to live on? Have you lost a parent or a child by their hands, and yourself the ruined and wretched survivor? If you have not, then are you not a judge of those who have. But if you have, and still can shake hands with the murderers, then are you unworthy the name of husband, father, friend, or lover, and whatever may be your rank or title in life, you have the heart of a coward, and the spirit of a sycophant.

This is not inflaming or exaggerating matters, but trying them by those feelings and affections which nature justifies, and without which, we should be incapable of discharging the social duties of life, or enjoying the felicities of it. I mean not to exhibit horror for the purpose of provoking revenge, but to awaken us from fatal and unmanly slumbers, that we may pursue determinately some fixed object. It is not in the power of Britain or of Europe to conquer America, if she do not conquer herself by *delay* and *timidity.* The present winter is worth an age if rightly employed, but if lost or neglected, the whole continent will partake of the misfortune; and there is no punishment which that man will not deserve, be he who, or what, or where he will, that may be the means of sacrificing a season so precious and useful.

It is repugnant to reason, to the universal order of things to all examples from former ages, to suppose, that this continent can longer remain subject to any external power. The most sanguine in Britain does not think so. The utmost stretch of human wisdom cannot, at this time, compass a plan short of separation, which can promise the continent even a year's security. Reconciliation is *now* a falacious dream. Nature hath deserted the connexion, and Art cannot supply her place. For, as Milton wisely expresses, "never can true reconcilement grow where wounds of deadly hate have pierced so deep."

Every quiet method for peace hath been ineffectual. Our prayers have been rejected with disdain; and only tended to convince us, that nothing flatters vanity, or confirms obstinacy in Kings more than repeated petitioning—and nothing hath contributed more than that very measure to make the Kings of Europe absolute: Witness Denmark and Sweden. Wherefore, since nothing but blows will do, for God's sake, let us come to a final separation, and not leave the next generation to be cutting throats, under the violated unmeaning names of parent and child.

To say, they will never attempt it again is idle and visionary, we thought so at the repeal of the stamp-act, yet a year or two undeceived us; as well may we suppose that nations, which have been once defeated, will never renew the quarrel.

As to government matters, it is not in the power of Britain to do this continent justice: The business of it will soon be too weighty, and intricate, to be managed with any tolerable degree of convenience, by a power, so distant from us, and so very ignorant of us; for if they cannot conquer us, they cannot govern us. To be always running three or four thousand miles with a tale or a petition, waiting four or five months for an answer, which when obtained requires five or six more to explain it in, will in a few years be looked upon as folly and child-ishness—There was a time when it was proper, and there is a proper time for it to cease.

Small islands not capable of protecting themselves, are the proper objects for kingdoms to take under their care; but there is something very absurd, in supposing a continent to be perpetually governed by an island. In no instance hath nature made the satellite larger than its primary planet, and as England and America, with respect to each other, reverses the common order of nature, it is evident they belong to different systems: England to Europe, America to itself.

I am not induced by motives of pride, party, or resentment to es-pouse the doctrine of separation and independance; I am clearly, pos-itively, and conscientiously persuaded that it is the true interest of this continent to be so; that every thing short of *that* is mere patchwork, that it can afford no lasting felicity,—that it is leaving the sword to our children, and shrinking back at a time, when, a little more, a little farther, would have rendered this continent the glory of the earth.

As Britain hath not manifested the least inclination towards a compromise, we may be assured that no terms can be obtained wor-thy the acceptance of the continent, or any ways equal to the expence of blood and treasure we have been already put to.

The object, contended for, ought always to bear some just propor-tion to the expence. The removal of North, or the whole detestable junto, is a matter unworthy the millions we have expended. A tempo-rary stoppage of trade, was an inconvenience, which would have suf-ficiently ballanced the repeal of all the acts complained of, had such repeals been obtained; but if the whole continent must take up arms, if every man must be a soldier, it is scarcely worth our while to fight against a contemptible ministry only. Dearly, dearly, do we pay for the repeal of the acts, if that is all we fight for; for in a just estimation, it is as great a folly to pay a Bunker-hill price for law, as for land. As I have always considered the independancy of this continent, as an event, which sooner or later must arrive, so from the late rapid progress of the continent to maturity, the event could not be far of. Wherefore, on the breaking out of hostilities, it was not worth the while to have disputed a matter, which time would have finally redressed, unless we meant to be in earnest; otherwise, it is like wasting an estate on a suit at law, to regulate the trespasses of a tenant, whose lease is just expiring. No man was a warmer wisher for reconciliation than myself, before the fatal nineteenth of April 1775*, but the moment the event of that day was made known, I rejected the hardened, sullen tempered Pharaoh of England for ever; and disdain the wretch, that with the pretended title of FATHER OF HIS PEOPLE can unfeelingly hear of their slaughter, and composedly sleep with their blood upon his soul.

But admitting that matters were now made up, what would be the event? I answer, the ruin of the continent. And that for several reasons.

First. The powers of governing still remaining in the hands of the king, he will have a negative over the whole legislation of this continent. And as he hath shewn himself such an inveterate enemy to liberty, and discovered such a thirst for arbitrary power; is he, or is he not, a proper man to say to these colonies, *"You shall make no laws but what I please."* And is there any inhabitant in America so ignorant, as not to know, that according to what is called the *present constitution,* that this continent can make no laws but what the king gives leave to; and is there any man so unwise, as not to see, that (considering what has happened) he will suffer no law to be made here, but such as suit *his* purpose. We may be as effectually enslaved by the want of laws in America, as by submitting to laws made for us in England. After matters are made up (as it is called) can there be any doubt, but the whole

---

* *Massacre at Lexington.*

power of the crown will be exerted, to keep this continent as low and humble as possible? Instead of going forward we shall go backward, or be perpetually quarrelling or ridiculously petitioning.—We are already greater than the king wishes us to be, and will he not here-after endeavour to make us less? To bring the matter to one point. Is the power who is jealous of our prosperity, a proper power to govern us? Whoever says *No* to this question is an *independant*, for indepen-dancy means no more, than, whether we shall make our own laws, or, whether the king, the greatest enemy this continent hath, or can have, shall tell us *"there shall be no laws but such as I like."*

But the king you will say has a negative in England; the people there can make no laws without his consent. In point of right and good order, there is something very ridiculous, that a youth of twenty-one (which hath often happened) shall say to several millions of people, older and wiser than himself, I forbid this or that act of yours to be law. But in this place I decline this sort of reply, though I will never cease to expose the absurdity of it, and only answer, that England being the King's residence, and America not so, make quite another case. The king's negative *here* is ten times more dangerous and fatal than it can be in England, for *there* he will scarcely refuse his consent to a bill for putting England into as strong a state of defence as possible, and in America he would never suffer such a bill to be passed.

America is only a secondary object in the system of British politics, England consults the good of *this* country, no farther than it answers her *own* purpose. Wherefore, her own interest leads her to suppress the growth of *ours* in every case which doth not promote her advan-tage, or in the least interferes with it. A pretty state we should soon be in under such a second-hand government, considering what has hap-pened! Men do not change from enemies to friends by the alteration of a name: And in order to shew that reconciliation *now* is a dangerous doctrine, I affirm, *that it would be policy in the king at this time, to repeal the acts for the sake of reinstating himself in the government of the provinces;* in order, that HE MAY ACCOMPLISH BY CRAFT AND SUB-TILTY, IN THE LONG RUN, WHAT HE CANNOT DO BY FORCE AND VIO-LENCE IN THE SHORT ONE. Reconciliation and ruin are nearly related.

Secondly. That as even the best terms, which we can expect to obtain, can amount to no more than a temporary expedient, or a kind of government by guardianship, which can last no longer than till the colonies come of age, so the general face and state of things, in the interim, will be unsettled and unpromising. Emigrants of property will not choose to come to a country whose form of government hangs but by a thread, and who is every day tottering on the brink of commotion and disturbance; and numbers of the present inhabitants would lay hold of the interval, to dispose of their effects, and quit the continent.

But the most powerful of all arguments, is, that nothing but independance, i. e. a continental form of government, can keep the peace of the continent and preserve it inviolate from civil wars. I dread the event of a reconciliation with Britain now, as it is more than probable, that it will be followed by a revolt somewhere or other, the consequences of which may be far more fatal than all the malice of Britain.

Thousands are already ruined by British barbarity; (thousands more will probably suffer the same fate) Those men have other feelings than us who have nothing suffered. All they *now* possess is liberty, what they before enjoyed is sacrificed to its service, and having nothing more to lose, they disdain submission. Besides, the general temper of the colonies, towards a British government, will be like that of a youth, who is nearly out of his time; they will care very little about her. And a government which cannot preserve the peace, is no government at all, and in that case we pay our money for nothing; and pray what is it that Britain can do, whose power will be wholly

on paper, should a civil tumult break out the very day after reconciliation? I have heard some men say, many of whom I believe spoke
without thinking, that they dreaded an independance, fearing that it
would produce civil wars. It is but seldom that our first thoughts are
truly correct, and that is the case here; for there are ten times more
to dread from a patched up connexion than from independance. I
make the sufferers case my own, and I protest, that were I driven from
house and home, my property destroyed, and my circumstances ruined, that as man, sensible of injuries, I could never relish the doctrine
of reconciliation, or consider myself bound thereby.

The colonies have manifested such a spirit of good order and obedience to continental government, as is sufficient to make every reasonable person easy and happy on that head. No man can assign the
least pretence for his fears, on any other grounds, than such as are
truly childish and ridiculous, viz. that one colony will be striving for
superiority over another.

Where there are no distinctions there can be no superiority, perfect equality affords no temptation. The republics of Europe are all
(and we may say always) in peace. Holland and Swisserland are without wars, foreign or domestic: Monarchical governments, it is true,
are never long at rest; the crown itself is a temptation to enterprising
ruffians at *home;* and that degree of pride and insolence ever atten-
dant on regal authority, swells into a rupture with foreign powers, in
instances, where a republican government, by being formed on more
natural principles, would negociate the mistake.

If there is any true cause of fear respecting independance, it is because no plan is yet laid down. Men do not see their way out—Wherefore, as an opening into that business, I offer the following hints; at
the same time modestly affirming, that I have no other opinion of
them myself, than that they may be the means of giving rise to something better. Could the straggling thoughts of individuals be collected,

they would frequently form materials for wise and able men to improve into useful matter.

Let the assemblies be annual, with a President only. The representation more equal. Their business wholly domestic, and subject to the authority of a Continental Congress.

Let each colony be divided into six, eight, or ten, convenient districts, each district to send a proper number of delegates to Congress, so that each colony send at least thirty. The whole number in Congress will be at least 390. Each Congress to sit   and to choose a president by the following method. When the delegates are met, let a colony be taken from the whole thirteen colonies by lot, after which, let the whole Congress choose (by ballot) a president from out of the delegates of *that* province. In the next Congress, let a colony be taken by lot from twelve only, omitting that colony from which the president was taken in the former Congress, and so proceeding on till the whole thirteen shall have had their proper rotation. And in order that nothing may pass into a law but what is satisfactorily just, not less than three fifths of the Congress to be called a majority.—He that will promote discord, under a government so equally formed as this, would have joined Lucifer in his revolt.

But as there is a peculiar delicacy, from whom, or in what manner, this business must first arise, and as it seems most agreeable and consistent that it should come from some intermediate body between the governed and the governors, that is, between the Congress and the people, let a CONTINENTAL CONFERENCE be held, in the following manner, and for the following purpose.

A committee of twenty-six members of Congress, viz. two for each colony. Two members from each House of Assembly, or Provincial Convention; and five representatives of the people at large, to be chosen in the capital city or town of each province, for, and in behalf of the whole province, by as many qualified voters as shall think proper to attend from all parts of the province for that purpose; or, if more convenient, the representatives may be chosen in two or three of the most populous parts thereof. In this conference, thus assembled, will be united, the two grand principles of business, *knowledge* and *power*. The members of Congress, Assemblies, or Conventions, by having had experience in national concerns, will be able and useful counsellors, and the whole, being impowered by the people, will have a truly legal authority.

The conferring members being met, let their business be to frame a CONTINENTAL CHARTER, or Charter of the United Colonies; (answering to what is called the Magna Charta of England) fixing the number and manner of choosing members of Congress, members of Assembly, with their date of sitting, and drawing the line of business and jurisdiction between them: (Always remembering, that our strength is continental, not provincial:) Securing freedom and property to all men, and above all things, the free exercise of religion, according to the dictates of conscience; with such other matter as is necessary for a charter to contain. Immediately after which, the said Conference to dissolve, and the bodies which shall be chosen conformable to the said charter, to be the legislators and governors of this continent for the time being: Whose peace and happiness, may God preserve, Amen.

Should any body of men be hereafter delegated for this or some similar purpose, I offer them the following extracts from that wise observer on governments *Dragonetti*. "The science" says he "of the politician consists in fixing the true point of happiness and freedom. Those men would deserve the gratitude of ages, who should discover a mode of government that contained the greatest sum of individual happiness, with the least national expence.

Dragonetti on virtue and rewards."

But where says some is the King of America? I'll tell you Friend, he reigns above, and doth not make havoc of mankind like the Royal Brute of Britain. Yet that we may not appear to be defective even in earthly honors, let a day be solemnly set apart for proclaiming the charter; let it be brought forth placed on the divine law, the word of God; let a crown be placed thereon, by which the world may know, that so far as we approve of monarchy, that in America THE LAW IS KING. For as in absolute governments the King is law, so in free countries the law *ought* to be King; and there ought to be no other. But lest any ill use should afterwards arise, let the crown at the conclusion of the ceremony be demolished, and scattered among the people whose right it is.

A government of our own is our natural right: And when a man seriously reflects on the precariousness of human affairs, he will become convinced, that it is finitely wiser and safer, to form a constitution of our own in a cool deliberate manner, while we have it in our power, than to trust such an interesting event to time and chance. If we omit it now, some* Massanello may hereafter arise, who laying hold of popular disquietudes, may collect together the desperate and the discontented, and by assuming to themselves the powers of government, may sweep away the liberties of the continent like a deluge. Should the government of America return again into the hands of Britain, the tottering situation of things, will be a temptation for some desperate adventurer to try his fortune; and in such a case, what relief can Britain give? Ere she could hear the news, the fatal business might be done; and ourselves suffering like the wretched Britons under the oppression of the Conqueror. Ye that oppose independance now, ye know not what ye do; ye are opening a door to eternal tyranny, by keeping vacant the seat of government. There are thousands,

---

* *Thomas Anello, otherwise Massanello, a fisherman of Naples, who after spiriting up his countrymen in the public market place, against the oppression of the Spaniards, to whom the place was then subject, prompted them to revolt, and in the space of a day became king.*

and tens of thousands, who would think it glorious to expel from the continent, that barbarous and hellish power, which hath stirred up the Indians and Negroes to destroy us, the cruelty hath a double guilt, it is dealing brutally by us, and treacherously by them.

To talk of friendship with those in whom our reason forbids us to have faith, and our affections wounded through a thousand pores instruct us to detest, is madness and folly. Every day wears out the little remains of kindred between us and them, and can there be any reason to hope, that as the relationship expires, the affection will increase, or that we shall agree better, when we have ten times more and greater concerns to quarrel over than ever?

Ye that tell us of harmony and reconciliation, can ye restore to us the time that is past? Can ye give to prostitution its former innocence? Neither can ye reconcile Britain and America. The last cord now is broken, the people of England are presenting addresses against us. There are injuries which nature cannot forgive; she would cease to be nature if she did. As well can the lover forgive the ravisher of his mistress, as the continent forgive the murders of Britain. The Almighty hath implanted in us these inextinguishable feelings for good and wise purposes. They are the guardians of his image in our hearts. They distinguish us from the herd of common animals. The social compact would dissolve, and justice be extirpated the earth, or have only a casual existence were we callous to the touches of affection. The robber, and the murderer, would often escape unpunished, did not the injuries which our tempers sustain, provoke us into justice.

O ye that love mankind! Ye that dare oppose, not only the tyranny, but the tyrant, stand forth! Every spot of the old world is overrun with oppression. Freedom hath been hunted round the globe. Asia, and Africa, have long expelled her.—Europe regards her like a stranger, and England hath given her warning to depart. O! receive the fugitive, and prepare in time an asylum for mankind.

Of the Present Ability of America, with Some Miscellaneous Reflexions.

I HAVE never met with a man, either in England or America, who hath not confessed his opinion, that a separation between the countries, would take place one time or other: And there is no instance, in which we have shewn less judgment, than in endeavouring to describe, what we call, the ripeness or fitness of the Continent for independance.

As all men allow the measure, and vary only in their opinion of the time, let us, in order to remove mistakes, take a general survey of things, and endeavour, if possible, to find out the *very* time. But we need not go far, the inquiry ceases at once, for, the *time hath found us.* The general concurrence, the glorious union of all things prove the fact.

It is not in numbers, but in unity, that our great strength lies; yet our present numbers are sufficient to repel the force of all the world.

The Continent hath, at this time, the largest body of armed and dis-
ciplined men of any power under Heaven; and is just arrived at that
pitch of strength, in which, no single colony is able to support itself,
and the whole, who united, can accomplish the matter, and either
more, or, less than this, might be fatal in its effects. Our land force is
already sufficient, and as to naval affairs, we cannot be insensible, that
Britain would never suffer an American man of war to be built, while
the continent remained in her hands. Wherefore, we should be no
forwarder an hundred years hence in that branch, than we are now;
but the truth is, we should be less so, because the timber of the country is every day diminishing, and that, which will remain at last, will
be far off and difficult to procure.

Were the continent crowded with inhabitants, her sufferings under
the present circumstances would be intolerable. The more sea port
towns we had, the more should we have both to defend and to loose.
Our present numbers are so happily proportioned to our wants, that
no man need be idle. The diminution of trade affords an army, and
the necessities of an army create a new trade.

Debts we have none; and whatever we may contract on this account will serve as a glorious memento of our virtue. Can we but
leave posterity with a settled form of government, an independant
constitution of it's own, the purchase at any price will be cheap. But
to expend millions for the sake of getting a few vile acts repealed, and
routing the present ministry only, is unworthy the charge, and is using posterity with the utmost cruelty; because it is leaving them the
great work to do, and a debt upon their backs, from which, they derive no advantage. Such a thought is unworthy a man of honor, and is
the true characteristic of a narrow heart and a pedling politician.

The debt we may contract doth not deserve our regard if the work
be but accomplished. No nation ought to be without a debt. A na-

tional debt is a national bond; and when it bears no interest, is in no case a grievance. Britain is oppressed with a debt of upwards of one hundred and forty millions sterling, for which she pays upwards of four millions interest. And as a compensation for her debt, she has a large navy; America is without a debt, and without a navy; yet for the twentieth part of the English national debt, could have a navy as large again. The navy of England is not worth, at this time, more than three millions and a half sterling.

The first and second editions of this pamphlet were published without the following calculations, which are now given as a proof that the above estimation of the navy is a just one. *See Entic's naval history, intro.* page 56.

The charge of building a ship of each rate, and furnishing her with masts, yards, sails and rigging, together with a proportion of eight months boatswain's and carpenter's sea-stores, as calculated by Mr. Burchett, Secretary to the navy.

	£.
For a ship of a 100 guns	35,553
90	29,886
80	23,638
70	17,785
60	14,197
50	10,606
40	7,558
30	5,846
20	3,710

And from hence it is easy to sum up the value, or cost rather, of the whole British navy, which in the year 1757, when it was at its greatest glory consisted of the following ships and guns.

Ships.	Guns.	Cost of one.	Cost of all.
6	100	35,553 *l.*	213,318 *l.*
12	90	29,886	358,632
12	80	23,638	283,656
43	70	17,785	764,755
35	60	14,197	496,895
40	50	10,606	424,240
45	40	7,558	340,110
58	20	3,710	215,180
85	Sloops, bombs, and fireships, one with another, at }	2,000	170,000
		Cost	3,266,786
	Remains for guns		233,214
			3,500,000

No country on the globe is so happily situated, so internally capable of raising a fleet as America. Tar, timber, iron, and cordage are her natural produce. We need go abroad for nothing. Whereas the Dutch, who make large profits by hiring out their ships of war to the Spaniards and Portuguese, are obliged to import most of the materials they use. We ought to view the building a fleet as an article of commerce, it being the natural manufactory of this country. It is the best money we can lay out. A navy when finished is worth more than it cost. And is that nice point in national policy, in which commerce and protection are united. Let us build; if we want them not, we can sell; and by that means replace our paper currency with ready gold and silver.

In point of manning a fleet, people in general run into great errors; it is not necessary that one fourth part should be sailors. The Terrible privateer, Captain Death, stood the hottest engagement of any ship last war, yet had not twenty sailors on board, though her complement of men was upwards of two hundred. A few able and social sailors will soon instruct a sufficient number of active landsmen in the com-

mon work of a ship. Wherefore, we never can be more capable to begin on maritime matters than now, while our timber is standing, our
fisheries blocked up, and our sailors and shipwrights out of employ.
Men of war, of seventy and eighty guns were built forty years ago in
New-England, and why not the same now? Ship-building is America's
greatest pride, and in which, she will in time excel the whole world.
The great empires of the east are mostly inland, and consequently ex-
cluded from the possibility of rivalling her. Africa is in a state of bar-
barism; and no power in Europe, hath either such an extent of coast,
or such an internal supply of materials. Where nature hath given the
one, she has withheld the other; to America only hath she been liberal
of both. The vast empire of Russia is almost shut out from the sea;
wherefore, her boundless forests, her tar, iron, and cordage are only
articles of commerce.

In point of safety, ought we to be without a fleet? We are not the
little people now, which we were sixty years ago; at that time we might
have trusted our property in the streets, or fields rather; and slept securely without locks or bolts to our doors or windows. The case now
is altered, and our methods of defence, ought to improve with our increase of property. A common pirate, twelve months ago, might have
come up the Delaware, and laid the city of Philadelphia under instant
contribution, for what sum he pleased; and the same might have happened to other places. Nay, any daring fellow, in a brig of fourteen or
sixteen guns, might have robbed the whole Continent, and carried off
half a million of money. These are circumstances which demand our
attention, and point out the necessity of naval protection.

Some, perhaps, will say, that after we have made it up with Britain,
she will protect us. Can we be so unwise as to mean, that she shall
keep a navy in our harbours for that purpose? Common sense will tell
us, that the power which hath endeavoured to subdue us, is of all others, the most improper to defend us. Conquest may be effected under

the pretence of friendship; and ourselves, after a long and brave resistance, be at last cheated into slavery. And if her ships are not to be admitted into our harbours, I would ask, how is she to protect us? A navy three or four thousand miles off can be of little use, and on sudden emergencies, none at all. Wherefore, if we must hereafter protect ourselves, why not do it for ourselves? Why do it for another?

The English list of ships of war, is long and formidable, but not a tenth part of them are at any one time fit for service, numbers of them not in being; yet their names are pompously continued in the list, if only a plank be left of the ship: and not a fifth part, of such as are fit for service, can be spared on any one station at one time. The East, and West Indies, Mediterranean, Africa, and other parts over which Britain extends her claim, make large demands upon her navy. From a mixture of prejudice and inattention, we have contracted a false notion respecting the navy of England, and have talked as if we should have the whole of it to encounter at once, and for that reason, supposed, that we must have one as large; which not being instantly practicable, have been made use of by a set of disguised Tories to discourage our beginning thereon. Nothing can be farther from truth than this; for if America had only a twentieth part of the naval force of Britain, she would be by far an over match for her; because, as we neither have, nor claim any foreign dominion, our whole force would be employed on our own coast, where we should, in the long run, have two to one the advantage of those who had three or four thousand miles to sail over, before they could attack us, and the same distance to return in order to refit and recruit. And although Britain by her fleet, hath a check over our trade to Europe, we have as large a one over her trade to the West-Indies, which, by laying in the neighbourhood of the Continent, is entirely at its mercy.

Some method might be fallen on to keep up a naval force in time of peace, if we should not judge it necessary to support a constant navy. If premiums were to be given to merchants, to build and employ in their service, ships mounted with twenty, thirty, forty, or fifty guns, (the premiums to be in proportion to the loss of bulk to the merchants) fifty or sixty of those ships, with a few guard ships on constant duty, would keep up a sufficient navy, and that without burdening ourselves with the evil so loudly complained of in England, of suffering their fleet, in time of peace to lie rotting in the docks. To unite the sinews of commerce and defence is sound policy; for when our strength and our riches, play into each other's hand, we need fear no external enemy.

In almost every article of defence we abound. Hemp flourishes even to rankness, so that we need not want cordage. Our iron is superior to that of other countries. Our small arms equal to any in the world. Cannon we can cast at pleasure. Saltpetre and gunpowder we are every day producing. Our knowledge is hourly improving. Resolution is our inherent character, and courage hath never yet forsaken us. Wherefore, what is it that we want? Why is it that we hesitate? From Britain we can expect nothing but ruin. If she is once admitted to the government of America again, this Continent will not be worth living in. Jealousies will be always arising; insurrections will be constantly happening; and who will go forth to quell them? Who will venture his life to reduce his own countrymen to a foreign obedience? The difference between Pennsylvania and Connecticut, respecting some unlocated lands, shews the insignificance of a British government, and fully proves, that nothing but Continental authority can regulate Continental matters.

Another reason why the present time is preferable to all others, is, that the fewer our numbers are, the more land there is yet unoccupied, which instead of being lavished by the king on his worthless dependants, may be hereafter applied, not only to the discharge of the present debt, but to the constant support of government. No nation under heaven hath such an advantage as this.

The infant state of the Colonies, as it is called, so far from being against, is an argument in favor of independance. We are sufficiently numerous, and were we more so, we might be less united. It is a matter worthy of observation, that the more a country is peopled, the smaller their armies are. In military numbers, the ancients far exceeded the moderns: and the reason is evident, for trade being the consequence of population, men become too much absorbed thereby to attend to anything else. Commerce diminishes the spirit, both of patriotism and military defence. And history sufficiently informs us, that the bravest achievements were always accomplished in the non-age of a nation. With the increase of commerce, England hath lost its spirit. The city of London, notwithstanding its numbers, submits to continued insults with the patience of a coward. The more men have to lose, the less willing are they to venture. The rich are in general slaves to fear, and submit to courtly power with the trembling duplicity of a Spaniel.

Youth is the seed time of good habits, as well in nations as in individuals. It might be difficult, if not impossible, to form the Continent into one government half a century hence. The vast variety of interests, occasioned by an increase of trade and population, would create confusion. Colony would be against colony. Each being able might scorn each other's assistance: and while the proud and foolish gloried in their little distinctions, the wise would lament, that the union had not been formed before. Wherefore, the *present time* is the *true time* for establishing it. The intimacy which is contracted in infancy, and the friendship which is formed in misfortune, are, of all others, the most lasting and unalterable. Our present union is marked with both these characters: we are young, and we have been distressed; but our concord hath withstood our troubles, and fixes a memorable æra for posterity to glory in.

The present time, likewise, is that peculiar time, which never happens to a nation but once, *viz.* the time of forming itself into a government. Most nations have let slip the opportunity, and by that means have been compelled to receive laws from their conquerors, instead of making laws for themselves. First, they had a king, and then a form of government; whereas, the articles or charter of government, should be formed first, and men delegated to execute them afterward: but from the errors of other nations, let us learn wisdom, and lay hold of the present opportunity—————*To begin government at the right end.*

When William the Conqueror subdued England, he gave them law at the point of the sword; and until we consent, that the seat of government, in America, be legally and authoritatively occupied, we shall be in danger of having it filled by some fortunate ruffian, who may treat us in the same manner, and then, where will be our freedom? where our property?

As to religion, I hold it to be the indispensible duty of all government, to protect all conscientious professors thereof, and I know of no other business which government hath to do therewith. Let a man throw aside that narrowness of soul, that selfishness of principle, which the niggards of all professions are so unwilling to part with, and he will be at once delivered of his fears on that head. Suspicion is the companion of mean souls, and the bane of all good society. For myself, I fully and conscientiously believe, that it is the will of the Almighty, that there should be diversity of religious opinions among us: It affords a larger field for our Christian kindness. Were we all of one way of thinking, our religious dispositions would want matter for probation; and on this liberal principle, I look on the various denominations among us, to be like children of the same family, differing only, in what is called, their Christian names.

In pages 34–35, I threw out a few thoughts on the propriety of a Continental Charter, (for I only presume to offer hints, not plans) and in this place, I take the liberty of rementioning the subject, by observing, that a charter is to be understood as a bond of solemn obligation, which the whole enters into, to support the right of every separate part, whether of religion, personal freedom, or property. A firm bargain and a right reckoning make long friends.

In a former page I likewise mentioned the necessity of a large and equal representation; and there is no political matter which more deserves our attention. A small number of electors, or a small number of representatives, are equally dangerous. But if the number of the representatives be not only small, but unequal, the danger is increased. As an instance of this, I mention the following; when the Associators petition was before the House of Assembly of Pennsylvania; twenty-eight members only were present, all the Bucks county members, being eight, voted against it, and had seven of the Chester members done the same, this whole province had been governed by two counties only, and this danger it is always exposed to. The unwarrantable stretch likewise, which that house made in their last sitting, to gain an undue authority over the Delegates of that province, ought to warn the people at large, how they trust power out of their own hands. A set of instructions for the Delegates were put together, which in point of sense and business would have dishonored a schoolboy, and after being approved by a *few*, a *very few* without doors, were carried into the House, and there passed *in behalf of the whole colony;* whereas, did the whole colony know, with what ill-will that House hath entered on some necessary public measures, they would not hesitate a moment to think them unworthy of such a trust.

Immediate necessity makes many things convenient, which if continued would grow into oppressions. Expedience and right are different things. When the calamities of America required a consultation, there was no method so ready, or at that time so proper, as to appoint persons from the several Houses of Assembly for that purpose; and the wisdom with which they have proceeded hath preserved this continent from ruin. But as it is more than probable that we shall never be without a CONGRESS, every well wisher to good order, must own, that the mode for choosing members of that body, deserves consideration. And I put it as a question to those, who make a study of mankind, whether *representation and election* is not too great a power for one and the same body of men to possess? When we are planning for posterity, we ought to remember, that virtue is not hereditary.

It is from our enemies that we often gain excellent maxims, and are frequently surprised into reason by their mistakes. Mr. Cornwall (one of the Lords of the Treasury) treated the petition of the New-York Assembly with contempt, because *that* House, he said, consisted but of twenty-six members, which trifling number, he argued, could not with decency be put for the whole. We thank him for his involuntary honesty.*

To CONCLUDE, however strange it may appear to some, or however unwilling they may be to think so, matters not, but many strong and striking reasons may be given, to shew, that nothing can settle our affairs so expeditiously as an open and determined declaration for independance. Some of which are,

First.—It is the custom of nations, when any two are at war, for some other powers, not engaged in the quarrel, to step in as mediators, and bring about the preliminaries of a peace: but while America calls herself the Subject of Great Britain, no power, however well disposed she may be, can offer her mediation. Wherefore, in our present state we may quarrel on for ever.

Secondly.—It is unreasonable to suppose, that France or Spain will give us any kind of assistance, if we mean only, to make use of that assistance for the purpose of repairing the breach, and strengthening

---

* *Those who would fully understand of what great consequence a large and equal representation is to a state, should read Burgh's political Disquisitions.*

the connection between Britain and America; because, those powers would be sufferers by the consequences.

Thirdly.—While we profess ourselves the subjects of Britain, we must, in the eye of foreign nations, be considered as rebels. The precedent is somewhat dangerous to *their peace,* for men to be in arms under the name of subjects; we, on the spot, can solve the paradox: but to unite resistance and subjection, requires an idea much too refined for common understanding.

Fourthly.—Were a manifesto to be published, and despatched to foreign courts, setting forth the miseries we have endured, and the peaceable methods we have ineffectually used for redress; declaring, at the same time, that not being able, any longer, to live happily or safely under the cruel disposition of the British court, we had been driven to the necessity of breaking off all connections with her; at the same time, assuring all such courts of our peaceable disposition towards them, and of our desire of entering into trade with them: Such a memorial would produce more good effects to this Continent, than if a ship were freighted with petitions to Britain.

Under our present denomination of British subjects, we can neither be received nor heard abroad: The custom of all courts is against us, and will be so, until, by an independance, we take rank with other nations.

These proceedings may at first appear strange and difficult; but, like all other steps which we have already passed over, will in a little time become familiar and agreeable; and, until an independance is declared, the Continent will feel itself like a man who continues putting off some unpleasant business from day to day, yet knows it must be done, hates to set about it, wishes it over, and is continually haunted with the thoughts of its necessity.

Appendix.

SINCE the publication of the first edition of this pamphlet, or rather, on the same day on which it came out, the King's Speech made its appearance in this city. Had the spirit of prophecy directed the birth of this production, it could not have brought it forth, at a more seasonable juncture, or a more necessary time. The bloody mindedness of the one, shew the necessity of pursuing the doctrine of the other. Men read by way of revenge. And the Speech, instead of terrifying, prepared a way for the manly principles of Independance.

Ceremony, and even, silence, from whatever motive they may arise, have a hurtful tendency, when they give the least degree of countenance to base and wicked performances; wherefore, if this maxim be admitted, it naturally follows, that the King's Speech, as being a piece of finished villany, deserved, and still deserves, a general execration both by the Congress and the people. Yet as the domestic tranquillity of a nation, depends greatly, on the *chastity* of what may properly be called NATIONAL MANNERS, it is often better, to pass some things over in silent disdain, than to make use of such new methods of dislike, as might introduce the least innovation, on that guardian of our peace and safety. And, perhaps, it is chiefly owing to this prudent delicacy, that the King's Speech, hath not, before now, suffered a public execution. The Speech if it may be called one, is nothing better than a wilful audacious libel against the truth, the common good, and the existence of mankind; and is a formal and pompous method of offering up human sacrifices to the pride of tyrants. But this general massacre of mankind, is one of the privileges, and the certain consequences of Kings; for as nature knows them *not,* they know *not her,* and although they are beings of our *own* creating, they know not *us,* and are become the gods of their creators. The Speech hath one good quality, which is, that it is not calculated to deceive, neither can we, even if we would, be deceived by it. Brutality and tyranny appear on the face of it. It leaves us at no loss: And every line convinces, even in the moment of reading, that He, who hunts the woods for prey, the naked and untutored Indian, is less a Savage than the King of Britain.

Sir John Dalrymple, the putative father of a whining jesuitical piece, fallaciously called, "*The Address of the people of* ENGLAND *to the inhabitants of* AMERICA," hath, perhaps, from a vain supposition, that the people *here* were to be frightened at the pomp and description of a king, given, (though very unwisely on his part) the real character of the present one: "But," says this writer, "if you are inclined to pay compliments to an administration, which we do not complain of," (meaning the Marquis of Rockingham's at the repeal of the Stamp Act) "it is very unfair in you to withhold them from that prince, *by whose* NOD ALONE *they were permitted to do any thing.*" This is toryism with a witness! Here is idolatry even without a mask: And he who can calmly hear, and digest such doctrine, hath forfeited his claim to rationality—an apostate from the order of manhood; and ought to be considered—as one, who hath not only given up the proper dignity of man, but sunk himself beneath the rank of animals, and contemptibly crawl through the world like a worm.

However, it matters very little now, what the king of England either says or does; he hath wickedly broken through every moral and human obligation, trampled nature and conscience beneath his feet; and by a steady and constitutional spirit of insolence and cruelty, procured for himself an universal hatred. It is *now* the interest of America to provide for herself. She hath already a large and young family, whom it is more her duty to take care of, than to be granting away her property, to support a power who is become a reproach to the names of men and christians—YE, whose office it is to watch over the morals of a nation, of whatsoever sect or denomination ye are of, as well as ye, who, are more immediately the guardians of the public liberty, if ye wish to preserve your native country uncontaminated by European corruption, ye must in secret wish a separation—But leaving the moral part to private reflection, I shall chiefly confine my farther remarks to the following heads.

First. That it is the interest of America to be separated from Britain.

Secondly. Which is the easiest and most practicable plan, RECONCILIATION OR INDEPENDANCE? with some occasional remarks.

In support of the first, I could, if I judged it proper, produce the opinion of some of the ablest and most experienced men on this continent; and whose sentiments, on that head, are not yet publicly known. It is in reality a self-evident position: For no nation in a state of foreign dependance, limited in its commerce, and cramped and fettered in its legislative powers, can ever arrive at any material eminence. America doth not yet know what opulence is; and although the progress which she hath made stands unparalleled in the history of other nations, it is but childhood, compared with what she would be capable of arriving at, had she, as she ought to have, the legislative powers in her own hands. England is, at this time, proudly coveting what would do her no good, were she to accomplish it; and the Continent hesitating on a matter, which will be her final ruin if neglected. It is the commerce and not the conquest of America, by which England is to be benefited, and that would in a great measure continue, were the countries as independant of each other as France and Spain; because in many articles, neither can go to a better market. But it is the independance of this country on Britain or any other, which is now the main and only object worthy of contention, and which, like all other truths discovered by necessity, will appear clearer and stronger every day.

First. Because it will come to that one time or other.

Secondly. Because, the longer it is delayed the harder it will be to accomplish.

I have frequently amused myself both in public and private companies, with silently remarking, the spacious errors of those who speak without reflecting. And among the many which I have heard, the following seems the most general, viz. that had this rupture happened forty or fifty years hence, instead of *now,* the Continent would have been more able to have shaken off the dependance. To which I reply, that our military ability, *at this time,* arises from the experience gained in the last war, and which in forty or fifty years time, would have been totally extinct. The Continent, would not, by that time, have had a General, or even a military officer left; and we, or those who may succeed us, would have been as ignorant of martial matters as the ancient Indians: And this single position, closely attended to, will unanswerably prove, that the present time is preferable to all others. The argument turns thus—at the conclusion of the last war, we had experience, but wanted numbers; and forty or fifty years hence, we should have numbers, without experience; wherefore, the proper

point of time, must be some particular point between the two ex-
tremes, in which a sufficiency of the former remains, and a proper
increase of the latter is obtained: And that point of time is the present
time.

The reader will pardon this digression, as it does not properly
come under the head I first set out with, and to which I again return
by the following position, viz.

Should affairs be patched up with Britain, and she to remain the
governing and sovereign power of America, (which, as matters are
now circumstanced, is giving up the point entirely) we shall deprive
ourselves of the very means of sinking the debt we have, or may contract. The value of the back lands which some of the provinces are
clandestinely deprived of, by the unjust extension of the limits of
Canada, valued only at five pounds sterling per hundred acres,
amount to upwards of twenty-five millions, Pennsylvania currency;
and the quit-rents at one penny sterling per acre, to two millions
yearly.

It is by the sale of those lands that the debt may be sunk, without
burthen to any, and the quit-rent reserved thereon, will always lessen,
and in time, will wholly support the yearly expence of government. It
matters not how long the debt is in paying, so that the lands when
sold be applied to the discharge of it, and for the execution of which,
the Congress for the time being, will be the continental trustees.

I proceed now to the second head, viz. Which is the earliest
and most practicable plan, RECONCILIATION OR INDEPENDANCE; with
some occasional remarks.

He who takes nature for his guide is not easily beaten out of his
argument, and on that ground, I answer *generally—That* INDEPEN-
DANCE *being a* SINGLE SIMPLE LINE, *contained within ourselves; and
reconciliation, a matter exceedingly perplexed and complicated, and in
which, a treacherous capricious court is to interfere, gives the answer
without a doubt.*

The present state of America is truly alarming to every man who is capable of reflexion. Without law, without government, without any other mode of power than what is founded on, and granted by courtesy. Held together by an unexampled concurrence of sentiment, which, is nevertheless subject to change, and which, every secret enemy is endeavouring to dissolve. Our present condition, is, Legislation without law; wisdom without a plan; a constitution without a name; and, what is strangely astonishing, perfect Independance contending for dependance. The instance is without a precedent; the case never existed before; and who can tell what may be the event? The property of no man is secure in the present unbraced system of things. The mind of the multitude is left at random, and seeing no fixed object before them, they pursue such as fancy or opinion starts. Nothing is criminal; there is no such thing as treason; wherefore, every one thinks himself at liberty to act as he pleases. The Tories dared not have assembled offensively, had they known that their lives, by that act, were forfeited to the laws of the state. A line of distinction should be drawn, between, English soldiers taken in battle, and inhabitants of America taken in arms. The first are prisoners, but the latter traitors. The one forfeits his liberty, the other his head.

Notwithstanding our wisdom, there is a visible feebleness in some of our proceedings which gives encouragement to dissensions. The Continental Belt is too loosely buckled. And if something is not done in time, it will be too late to do any thing, and we shall fall into a state, in which, neither *Reconciliation* nor *Independance* will be practicable. The king and his worthless adherents are got at their old game of dividing the Continent, and there are not wanting among us, Printers, who will be busy in spreading specious falsehoods. The artful and hypocritical letter which appeared a few months ago in two of the New-York papers, and likewise in two others, is an evidence that there are men who want either judgment or honesty.

It is easy getting into holes and corners and talking of reconciliation: But do such men seriously consider, how difficult the task is, and how dangerous it may prove, should the Continent divide thereon. Do they take within their view, all the various orders of men whose situation and circumstances, as well as their own, are to be considered therein. Do they put themselves in the place of the sufferer whose *all* is *already* gone, and of the soldier, who hath quitted *all* for the defence of his country. If their ill judged moderation be suited to their own private situations *only*, regardless of others, the event will convince them, that "they are reckoning without their Host."

Put us, says some, on the footing we were on in sixty-three: To which I answer, the request is not *now* in the power of Britain to comply with, neither will she propose it; but if it were, and even should be granted, I ask, as a reasonable question, By what means is such a corrupt and faithless court to be kept to its engagements? Another parliament, nay, even the present, may hereafter repeal the obligation, on the pretence, of its being violently obtained, or unwisely granted; and in that case, Where is our redress?—No going to law with nations; cannon are the barristers of Crowns; and the sword, not of justice, but of war, decides the suit. To be on the footing of sixty-three, it is not sufficient, that the laws only be put on the same state, but, that our circumstances, likewise, be put on the same state; Our burnt and destroyed towns repaired or built up, our private losses made good, our public debts (contracted for defence) discharged; otherwise, we shall be millions worse than we were at that enviable period. Such a request, had it been complied with a year ago, would have won the heart and soul of the Continent—but now it is too late, "The Rubicon is passed."

Besides, the taking up arms, merely to enforce the repeal of a pecuniary law, seems as unwarrantable by the divine law, and as repugnant to human feelings, as the taking up arms to enforce obedience thereto. The object, on either side, doth not justify the means; for the lives of men are too valuable to be cast away on such trifles. It is the violence which is done and threatened to our persons; the destruction of our property by an armed force; the invasion of our country by fire and sword, which conscientiously qualifies the use of arms: And the instant, in which such a mode of defence became necessary, all subjection to Britain ought to have ceased; and the independancy of America, should have been considered, as dating its æra from, and published by, *the first musket that was fired against her.* This line is a line of consistency; neither drawn by caprice, nor extended by ambition; but produced by a chain of events, of which the colonies were not the authors.

I shall conclude these remarks, with the following timely and well intended hints, We ought to reflect, that there are three different ways, by which an independancy may hereafter be effected; and that *one* of those *three,* will one day or other, be the fate of America, viz. By the legal voice of the people in Congress; by a military power; or by a mob: It may not always happen that our soldiers are citizens, and the multitude a body of reasonable men; virtue, as I have already remarked, is not hereditary, neither is it perpetual. Should an independancy be brought about by the first of those means, we have every opportunity and every encouragement before us, to form the noblest purest constitution on the face of the earth. We have it in our power to begin the world over again. A situation, similar to the present, hath not happened since the days of Noah until now. The birthday of a new world is at hand, and a race of men, perhaps as numerous as all Europe contains, are to receive their portion of freedom from the event of a few months. The Reflexion is awful—and in this point of view, How trifling, how ridiculous, do the little, paltry cavellings, of a few weak or interested men appear, when weighed against the business of a world.

Should we neglect the present favorable and inviting period, and an Independance be hereafter effected by any other means, we must charge the consequence to ourselves, or to those rather, whose narrow and prejudiced souls, are habitually opposing the measure, without either inquiring or reflecting. There are reasons to be given in support of Independance, which men should rather privately think of, than be publicly told of. We ought not now to be debating whether we shall be independant or not, but, anxious to accomplish it on a firm, secure, and honorable basis, and uneasy rather that it is not yet began upon. Every day convinces us of its necessity. Even the Tories (if such beings yet remain among us) should, of all men, be the most solicitous to promote it; for, as the appointment of committees at first, protected them from popular rage, so, a wise and well established form of government, will be the only certain means of continuing it securely to them. *Wherefore,* if they have not virtue enough to be Whigs, they ought to have prudence enough to wish for Independance.

In short, Independance is the only Bond that can tye and keep us together. We shall then see our object, and our ears will be legally shut against the schemes of an intriguing, as well, as a cruel enemy. We shall then too, be on a proper footing, to treat with Britain; for there is reason to conclude, that the pride of that court, will be less hurt by treating with the American states for terms of peace, than with those, whom she denominates, "rebellious subjects," for terms of accommodation. It is our delaying it that encourages her to hope for conquest, and our backwardness tends only to prolong the war. As we have, without any good effect therefrom, withheld our trade to obtain a redress of our grievances, let us *now* try the alternative, by *independantly* redressing them ourselves, and then offering to open the trade. The mercantile and reasonable part of England, will be still with us; because, peace *with* trade, is preferable to war *without* it. And if this offer be not accepted, other courts may be applied to.

On these grounds I rest the matter. And as no offer hath yet been made to refute the doctrine contained in the former editions of this pamphlet, it is a negative proof, that either the doctrine cannot be refuted, or, that the party in favour of it are too numerous to be opposed. WHEREFORE, instead of gazing at each other with suspicious or doubtful curiosity, let each of us, hold out to his neighbour the hearty hand of friendship, and unite in drawing a line, which, like an act of oblivion shall bury in forgetfulness every former dissention. Let the names of Whig and Tory be extinct; and let none other be heard among us, than those of *a good citizen, an open and resolute friend, and a virtuous supporter of the* RIGHTS *of* MANKIND *and of the* FREE AND INDEPENDANT STATES OF AMERICA.

To the Representatives of the Religious Society of the People called Quakers, or to so many of them as were concerned in publishing a late piece, entitled "The ANCIENT TESTIMONY and PRINCIPLES of the People called QUAKERS renewed, with Respect to the KING and GOVERNMENT, and touching the COMMOTIONS now prevailing in these and other parts of AMERICA addressed to the PEOPLE IN GENERAL."

THE Writer of this, is one of those few, who never dishonors religion either by ridiculing, or cavilling at any denomination whatsoever. To God, and not to man, are all men accountable on the score of religion. Wherefore, this epistle is not so properly addressed to you as a religious, but as a political body, dabbling in matters, which the professed Quietude of your Principles instruct you not to meddle with.

As you have, without a proper authority for so doing, put yourselves in the place of the whole body of the Quakers, so, the writer of this, in order to be on an equal rank with yourselves, is under the necessity, of putting himself in the place of all those, who, approve the very writings and principles, against which, your testimony is directed: And he hath chosen this singular situation, in order, that you might discover in him that presumption of character which you cannot see in yourselves. For neither he nor you have any claim or title to *Political Representation*.

When men have departed from the right way, it is no wonder that they stumble and fall. And it is evident from the manner in which ye have managed your testimony, that politics, (as a religious body of men) is not your proper Walk; for however well adapted it might appear to you, it is, nevertheless, a jumble of good and bad put unwisely together, and the conclusion drawn therefrom, both unnatural and unjust.

The two first pages, (and the whole doth not make four) we give you credit for, and expect the same civility from you, because the love and desire of peace is not confined to Quakerism, it is the *natural,* as well the religious wish of all denominations of men. And on this ground, as men laboring to establish an Independant Constitution of our own, do we exceed all others in our hope, end, and aim. *Our plan is peace for ever.* We are tired of contention with Britain, and can see no real end to it but in a final separation. We act consistently, because for the sake of introducing an endless and uninterrupted peace, do we bear the evils and burthens of the present day. We are endeavoring, and will steadily continue to endeavor, to separate and dissolve a connexion which hath already filled our land with blood; and which, while the name of it remains, will be the fatal cause of future mischiefs to both countries.

We fight neither for revenge nor conquest; neither from pride nor passion; we are not insulting the world with our fleets and armies, nor ravaging the globe for plunder. Beneath the shade of our own vines are we attacked; in our own houses, and on our own lands, is the violence committed against us. We view our enemies in the character of Highwaymen and Housebreakers, and having no defence for ourselves in the civil law, are obliged to punish them by the military one, and apply the sword, in the very case, where you have before now, applied the halter————————Perhaps we feel for the ruined and insulted sufferers in all and every part of the continent, with a degree of tenderness which hath not yet made it's way into some of your bosoms. But be ye sure that ye mistake not the cause and ground of your Testimony. Call not coldness of soul, religion; nor put the *Bigot* in the place of the *Christian.*

O ye partial ministers of your own acknowledged principles. If the bearing arms be sinful, the first going to war must be more so, by all the difference between wilful attack and unavoidable defence. Wherefore, if ye really preach from conscience, and mean not to make a political hobby-horse of your religion, convince the world thereof, by proclaiming your doctrine to our enemies, *for they likwise bear* ARMS. Give us proof of your sincerity by publishing it at St. James's, to the commanders in chief at Boston, to the Admirals and Captains who are piratically ravaging our coasts, and to all the murdering miscreants who are acting in authority under HIM whom ye profess to serve. Had ye the honest soul of* *Barclay* ye would preach repentance to *your* king; Ye would tell the Royal Wretch his sins, and warn him of eternal ruin. Ye would not spend your partial invectives against the injured and the insulted only, but, like faithful ministers, would cry aloud and *spare none.* Say not that ye are persecuted, neither endeav-

---

* *"Thou hast tasted of prosperity and adversity: thou knowest what it is to be banished thy native country, to be over-ruled as well as to rule, and set upon the throne; and being* oppressed *thou hast reason to know how* hateful *the* oppressor *is both to God and man: If after all these warnings and advertisements, thou dost not turn unto the Lord with all thy heart, but forget him who remembered thee in thy distress, and give up thyself to follow lust and vanity, surely great will be thy condemnation.—Against which snare, as well as the temptation of those who may or do feed thee, and prompt thee to evil, the most excellent and prevalent remedy will be, to apply thyself to that light of Christ which shineth in thy conscience, and which neither can, nor will flatter thee, nor suffer thee to be at ease in thy sins."*

Barclay's Address to Charles II.

our to make us the authors of that reproach, which, ye are bringing upon yourselves; for we testify unto all men, that we do not complain against you because ye are *Quakers,* but because ye pretend to *be* and are NOT Quakers.

Alas! it seems by the particular tendency of some part of your testimony, and other parts of your conduct, as if, all sin was reduced to, and comprehended in, *the act of bearing arms,* and that by the *people only.* Ye appear to us, to have mistaken party for conscience; because, the general tenor of your actions wants uniformity: And it is exceedingly difficult to us to give credit to many of your pretended scruples; because, we see them made by the same men, who, in the very instant that they are exclaiming against the mammon of this world, are nevertheless, hunting after it with a step as steady as Time, and an appetite as keen as Death.

The quotation which ye have made from Proverbs, in the third page of your testimony, that, "when a man's ways please the Lord, he maketh even his enemies to be at peace with him"; is very unwisely chosen on your part; because, it amounts to a proof, that the king's ways (whom ye are so desirous of supporting) do *not* please the Lord, otherwise, his reign would be in peace.

I now proceed to the latter part of your testimony, and that, for which all the foregoing seems only an introduction, viz.

"It hath ever been our judgment and principle, since we were called to profess the light of Christ Jesus, manifested in our consciences unto this day, that the sitting up and putting down kings and governments, is God's peculiar prerogative; for causes best known to himself: And that it is not our business to have any hand or contrivance therein; nor to be busy bodies above our station, much less to plot and contrive the ruin, or overturn of any of them, but to pray for the king, and safety of our nation, and good of all men: That we may live a peaceable and quiet life, in all godliness and honesty; *under the government which God is pleased to set over us."*—If these are *really* your principles why do ye not abide by them? Why do ye not leave that, which ye call God's Work, to be managed by himself? These very principles instruct you to wait with patience and humility, for the event of all public measures, and to receive *that event* as the divine will towards you. *Wherefore,* what occasion is there for your *political testimony* if you fully believe what it contains? And the very publishing it proves, that either, ye do not believe what ye profess, or have not virtue enough to practice what ye believe.

The principles of Quakerism have a direct tendency to make a man the quiet and inoffensive subject of any, and every government *which is set over him.* And if the setting up and putting down of kings and governments is God's peculiar prerogative, he most certainly will not be robbed thereof by us; wherefore, the principle itself leads you to approve of every thing, which ever happened, or may happen to kings as being his work. OLIVER CROMWELL thanks you. CHARLES, then, died not by the hands of man; and should the present Proud Imitator of him, come to the same untimely end, the writers and publishers of the Testimony, are bound, by the doctrine it contains, to applaud the fact. Kings are not taken away by miracles, neither are changes in governments brought about by any other means than such as are common and human; and such as we are now using. Even the dispersion of the Jews, though foretold by our Saviour, was effected by arms. Wherefore, as ye refuse to be the means on one side, ye ought not to be meddlers on the other; but to wait the issue in silence; and unless you can produce divine authority, to prove, that the Almighty who hath created and placed this *new* world, at the greatest distance it could possibly stand, east and west, from every part of the old, doth, nevertheless, disapprove of its being independent of the corrupt and abandoned court of Britain, unless I say, ye can shew this, how can ye on the ground of your principles, justify the exciting and stirring up the people "firmly to unite in the *abhorrence* of all such *writings*, and *measures*, as evidence a desire and design to break off the *happy* connexion we have hitherto enjoyed, with the kingdom of Great-Britain, and our just and necessary subordination to the king, and those who are lawfully placed in authority under him." What a slap of the face is here! the men, who, in the very paragraph before, have quietly and passively resigned up the ordering, altering, and disposal of kings and governments, into the hands of God, are now, recalling their principles, and putting in for a share of the business. Is it possible, that the conclusion, which is here justly quoted, can any ways follow from the doctrine laid down? The inconsistency is too glaring not to be seen; the absurdity too great not to be laughed at; and such as could only have been made by those, whose understandings were darkened by the narrow and crabby spirit of a dispairing political party; for ye are not to be considered as the whole body of the Quakers but only as a factional and fractional part thereof.

Here ends the examination of your testimony; (which I call upon no man to abhor, as ye have done, but only to read and judge of fairly;) to which I subjoin the following remark; "That the setting up and putting down of kings," most certainly mean, the making him a king, who is yet not so, and the making him no king who is already one. And pray what hath this to do in the present case? We neither mean to *set up* nor to *put down*, neither to *make* nor to *unmake*, but to have nothing to *do* with them. Wherefore, your testimony in whatever light it is viewed serves only to dishonor your judgment, and for many other reasons had better have been let alone than published.

First, Because it tends to the decrease and reproach of all religion whatever, and is of the utmost danger to society, to make it a party in political disputes.

Secondly, Because it exhibits a body of men, numbers of whom disavow the publishing political testimonies, as being concerned therein and approvers thereof.

Thirdly, Because it hath a tendency to undo that continental harmony and friendship which yourselves by your late liberal and charitable donations hath lent a hand to establish; and the preservation of which, is of the utmost consequence to us all.

And here without anger or resentment I bid you farewell. Sincerely wishing, that as men and christians, ye may always fully and uninterruptedly enjoy every civil and religious right; and be, in your turn, the means of securing it to others; but that the example which ye have unwisely set, of mingling religion with politics, *may be disavowed and reprobated by every inhabitant of* AMERICA.

FINIS.

Selected Bibliography

Paine's Writings

Conway, Moncure Daniel, ed. *The Writings of Thomas Paine*. New York: G. P. Putnam's Sons, 1894–1896.

Foner, Philip S., ed. *The Complete Writings of Thomas Paine*. New York: Citadel Press, 1945.

Foot, Michael, and Isaac Kramnick, eds. *The Thomas Paine Reader*. London: Penguin, 1987.

Biographies

Aldridge, Alfred Owen. *Man of Reason: The Life of Thomas Paine*. Philadelphia: J. B. Lippincott, 1959.

Foner, Eric. *Tom Paine and Revolutionary America*. New York: Oxford University Press, 1976.

Fruchtman, Jack, Jr. *Thomas Paine: Apostle of Freedom*. New York: Four Walls, Eight Windows, 1994.

Hawke, David Freeman. *Paine*. New York: W. W. Norton, 1974.

Keane, John. *Tom Paine: A Political Life.* Boston: Little Brown, 1995.

Nelson, Craig. *Thomas Paine: Enlightenment, Revolution, and the Birth of Modern Nations.* New York: Viking, 2006.

Williamson, Audrey. *Thomas Paine: His Life, Work, and Times.* London: George Allen and Unwin, 1973.

Critical Studies

Aldridge, Alfred Owen. *Thomas Paine's American Ideology.* Newark: University of Delaware Press, 1984.

Appleby, Joyce O. *Liberalism and Republicanism in the Historical Imagination.* Cambridge, Mass.: Harvard University Press, 1992.

Claeys, Gregory. *Thomas Paine's Social and Political Thought.* Winchester, Mass.: Unwin Hyman, 1989.

Davidson, Edward H., and William J. Scheick. *Paine, Scripture, and Authority: The Age of Reason as Religious and Political Idea.* Bethlehem, Penn.: Lehigh University Press, 1994.

Durey, Michael. *Transatlantic Radicals and the Early American Republic.* Lawrence: University of Kansas Press, 1997.

Fruchtman, Jack, Jr. *The Political Philosophy of Thomas Paine.* Baltimore: Johns Hopkins University Press, 2009.

Gay, Peter. *The Enlightenment: An Interpretation.* 2 vols. New York: W. W. Norton, 1996–1997.

Jordan, Winthrop D. "Familial Politics: Thomas Paine and the Killing of the King, 1776." *Journal of American History* 60 (1973): 294–308.

Kaye, Harvey J. *Thomas Paine and the Promise of America.* New York: Hill and Wang, 2005.

Kramnick, Isaac. *Republicanism and Bourgeois Radicalism: Political Ideology in Late Eighteenth-Century England and America.* Ithaca, N.Y.: Cornell University Press, 1990.

Moore, Judy. *Thomas Paine's Lewes.* Seaford, Eng.: S. B. Publications, 2000.

Thompson, E. P. *The Making of the English Working Class.* New York: Vintage, 1966.

Wilson, David A. *Paine and Cobbett: The Transatlantic Connection.* Montreal: McGill-Queen's University Press, 1988.

Wood, Gordon S. *The Radicalism of the American Revolution.* New York: Alfred A. Knopf, 1992.